GREAT TASTING
STIR-FRIES
AND MORE

PUBLICATIONS INTERNATIONAL, LTD.

GREAT TASTING
STIR-FRIES
AND MORE

STIR-FRY ESSENTIALS

Stir-fry cooking—the art of rapidly cooking small pieces of food over high heat, usually in hot oil—is most often associated with Asian cuisines. **Great Tasting Stir-Fries and More** will convince you that the versatile stir-frying technique extends far beyond the Orient and works wonderfully with a wide variety of ingredients. This exciting new publication offers over 90 delicious opportunities to experience a vast assortment of tempting stir-fried creations, from exotic-tasting classic Chinese dishes to bold new flavor combinations reminiscent of Italian, Tex-Mex or spa cooking. Stir-frying lends itself to quick and nutritious menus while maximizing the flavors and textures of your ingredients. Read on for guidelines guaranteed to make your stir-fries an unforgettable success every time.

Here's a hot tip to keep in mind: Before beginning any recipe, read it all the way through at least once so you know what to expect and are sure not to miss any steps!

Getting Ready

Stir-frying can be broken down into two separate steps: (1) preparation of ingredients; and, (2) cooking. Because stir-frying requires constant attention during a relatively short cooking time, all ingredients should be cleaned, cut up, measured and arranged for easy access before you begin cooking. If possible, use different cutting boards for meats and vegetables (or wash the cutting board between uses with warm, soapy water). Knives should also be thoroughly cleaned after cutting raw meat, poultry and seafood. These precautions limit the possibility of spreading harmful bacteria between ingredients. To guarantee that meats and vegetables cook evenly, cut them into equal-sized pieces according to the recipe directions. Also, it may be easier to thinly slice meat and poultry that has been partially frozen first.

Heavy-duty resealable plastic food storage bags are perfect for marinating ingredients. Any foods marinated longer than 20 minutes should be marinated in the refrigerator. To prevent lumping, make sure to stir any mixtures containing cornstarch immediately before using.

Cook It Up

A wok is usually used for stir-frying, although a large, heavy skillet can work just as well. Because a wok has high, sloping sides, there is ample hot surface area to ensure even cooking. Also, the vigorously stirred and tossed ingredients are easily contained by a high-sided pan. Many kinds of woks are available: round- or flat-bottomed woks made of thin or heavy rolled steel, aluminum, stainless steel or copper as well as electric woks with nonstick finishes and thermostatic controls. Whichever type of wok you use, be sure to follow the manufacturer's instructions for using and taking care of it. Woks range widely in size from 12 to 24 inches in diameter. A 14-inch wok is an ideal choice because it can accommodate the typical amounts of ingredients without taking up too much space on the stove.

Remember: You can successfully stir-fry a little food in a large wok (or skillet) but a lot of food in a little wok will bring disappointing results.

The kind of oil used for stir-frying is also very important. Use vegetable oils such as peanut, corn, canola, soybean or a combination of these oils because they withstand high heat without smoking. Sesame oil, olive oil and butter burn easily.

When the ingredients are ready to go and you're set to cook, heat the wok until it's very hot. Next, add the oil; it takes only about 30 seconds to heat thoroughly when added to a hot pan. Usually, the meat, poultry or seafood is stir-fried first and removed from the wok. Then the vegetables are added to the wok, followed by the sauce. Finally, the meat is added back to finish cooking or just heat through.

Note: Because the choices of ingredients, heat sources and cooking equipment can vary greatly from reader to reader, the cooking times given in the recipes of this publication should be considered guidelines.

SALADS & STARTERS

CHINATOWN STUFFED MUSHROOMS

24 large fresh mushrooms (about
   1 pound), cleaned and
   stems trimmed
½ pound ground turkey
1 clove garlic, minced
¼ cup fine dry bread crumbs
¼ cup thinly sliced green onions

3 tablespoons reduced-sodium
   soy sauce, divided
1 teaspoon minced fresh ginger
1 egg white, slightly beaten
⅛ teaspoon crushed red pepper
   flakes (optional)

Remove stems from mushrooms; finely chop enough stems to equal 1 cup. Cook turkey with chopped stems and garlic in medium skillet over medium-high heat until turkey is no longer pink, stirring to separate turkey. Spoon off any fat. Stir in bread crumbs, green onions, 2 tablespoons soy sauce, ginger, egg white and crushed red pepper; mix well.

Brush mushroom caps lightly on all sides with remaining 1 tablespoon soy sauce; spoon about 2 teaspoons stuffing into each mushroom cap.* Place stuffed mushrooms on rack of foil-lined broiler pan. Broil 4 to 5 inches from heat 5 to 6 minutes or until hot. *Makes 24 appetizers*

*Mushrooms may be made ahead to this point; cover and refrigerate up to 24 hours. Add 1 to 2 minutes to broiling time for chilled mushrooms.

Chinatown Stuffed Mushrooms

Holland House® Stir-Fry Sauce

HOLLAND HOUSE® STIR–FRY SAUCE

1 teaspoon vegetable oil
1 bunch scallions, thinly sliced
2 cloves garlic, minced
¼ teaspoon ground ginger
¾ cup HOLLAND HOUSE®
　Sherry Cooking Wine
1 tablespoon reduced-sodium
　or regular soy sauce

1 cup reduced-sodium chicken
　broth
2 tablespoons cornstarch
1 to 2 tablespoons toasted
　sesame seeds (optional)

In medium saucepan, heat oil and cook scallions, garlic and ginger until scallions are just tender, about 4 minutes. Stir in Holland House® Cooking Wine, soy sauce and broth blended with cornstarch. Bring to a boil and stir 1 minute.

Serve as a sauce for grilled or broiled vegetables, steamed vegetables or with your favorite stir-fry recipe. Sprinkle with toasted sesame seeds, if desired.

Makes about 2 cups

STIR-FRIED BEEF & EGGPLANT SALAD

½ pound boneless tender beef
    steak (sirloin, rib eye or top
    loin)
⅓ cup KIKKOMAN® Stir-Fry
    Sauce
1 teaspoon distilled white
    vinegar
¼ to ½ teaspoon crushed red
    pepper
1 clove garlic, pressed
    Lettuce leaves (optional)

3 cups finely shredded iceberg
    lettuce
3 tablespoons vegetable oil,
    divided
1 medium eggplant, cut into
    julienne strips
1 medium carrot, cut into
    julienne strips
6 green onions, cut into
    1½-inch lengths, separating
    whites from tops

Cut beef across grain into thin slices, then into strips. Combine stir-fry sauce, vinegar, red pepper and garlic. Coat beef with 1 tablespoon of the stir-fry sauce mixture; set aside remaining mixture. Line edge of large shallow bowl or large platter with lettuce leaves; arrange shredded lettuce in center. Heat 1 tablespoon oil in hot wok or large skillet over high heat. Add beef and stir-fry 1 minute; remove. Heat remaining 2 tablespoons oil in same pan; add eggplant and stir-fry 6 minutes. Add carrot and white parts of green onions; stir-fry 3 minutes. Add green onion tops; stir-fry 2 minutes longer. Add remaining stir-fry sauce mixture and beef. Cook and stir just until beef and vegetables are coated with sauce. Spoon mixture over shredded lettuce; toss well to combine before serving. Serve immediately. *Makes 2 to 3 servings*

STIR-FRIED SHRIMP APPETIZERS

¼ cup KIKKOMAN® Soy Sauce
¼ cup dry white wine
¼ cup chopped green onions
1 clove garlic, pressed
1 teaspoon ground ginger

1 pound medium-size raw
    shrimp, peeled and
    deveined
3 tablespoons vegetable oil

Combine soy sauce, wine, green onions, garlic and ginger; stir in shrimp and let stand 15 minutes. Heat oil in hot wok or large skillet over medium-high heat. Drain shrimp and add to pan. Discard marinade. Stir-fry 1 to 2 minutes, or until shrimp are pink. Serve immediately. *Makes 8 servings*

ORIENTAL SALSA

1 cup diced unpeeled
   cucumber
½ cup chopped red bell pepper
½ cup thinly sliced green onions
⅓ cup coarsely chopped
   cilantro
1 clove garlic, minced
2 tablespoons reduced-sodium
   soy sauce

1 tablespoon rice vinegar
½ teaspoon Oriental sesame oil
¼ teaspoon crushed red pepper
   flakes
Easy Wonton Chips (recipe
   follows) or assorted fresh
   vegetables for dipping

Combine cucumber, bell pepper, onions, cilantro, garlic, soy sauce, rice vinegar, oil and crushed red pepper in medium bowl until well blended. Cover and refrigerate until serving time. Serve with Easy Wonton Chips or assorted fresh vegetables for dipping. Or, use as an accompaniment to broiled fish, chicken or pork.   *Makes 1½ cups salsa*

EASY WONTON CHIPS

1 tablespoon soy sauce
2 teaspoons vegetable oil
½ teaspoon sugar

¼ teaspoon garlic salt
12 wonton wrappers
   Nonstick cooking spray

Preheat oven to 375°F. Combine soy sauce, oil, sugar and garlic salt in small bowl; mix well. Cut each wonton wrapper diagonally in half. Place on 15×10-inch jelly-roll pan coated with nonstick cooking spray. Brush soy mixture lightly but evenly over both sides of wrappers. Bake 4 to 6 minutes or until crisp and lightly browned, turning after 3 minutes. Transfer to cooling rack; cool completely.   *Makes 2 dozen chips*

BITS O' TERIYAKI CHICKEN

½ cup KIKKOMAN® Teriyaki
   Sauce
1 teaspoon sugar
2 whole chicken breasts,
   skinned and boned

1 teaspoon cornstarch
1 tablespoon water
1 tablespoon vegetable oil
2 tablespoons sesame seed,
   toasted

Combine teriyaki sauce and sugar in small bowl. Cut chicken into 1-inch pieces; stir into teriyaki sauce mixture. Marinate 30 minutes, stirring occasionally. Remove chicken; reserve 2 tablespoons marinade. Combine reserved marinade, cornstarch and water in small bowl; set aside. Heat oil in hot wok or large skillet over medium-high heat. Add chicken and sesame seed; stir-fry 2 minutes. Stir in cornstarch mixture. Cook and stir until mixture boils and thickens and chicken is tender, about 1 minute. Turn into chafing dish or onto serving platter. Serve warm with wooden picks.

Makes 6 servings

CREAM OF PUMPKIN CURRY SOUP

3 tablespoons butter
1 cup chopped onion
1 clove garlic, peeled and finely
   chopped
1 teaspoon curry powder
½ teaspoon salt
⅛ to ¼ teaspoon ground
   coriander
⅛ teaspoon crushed red pepper
   flakes

3 cups water
3 MAGGI® Vegetarian
   Vegetable Bouillon Cubes
1¾ cups (15- or 16-ounce can)
   LIBBY'S® Solid Pack
   Pumpkin
1 cup half-and-half
   Sour cream and chopped
   fresh chives (optional)

Melt butter in large saucepan. Add onion and garlic; cook and stir 3 to 5 minutes or until soft. Stir in curry powder, salt, coriander and red pepper flakes; cook 1 minute. Add water and bouillon cubes; bring to a boil. Reduce heat; cook gently, stirring occasionally, 15 to 20 minutes. Stir in pumpkin and half-and-half; cook 5 minutes.

Pour pumpkin mixture into food processor or blender container. Cover; process until creamy. Serve warm or reheat to desired temperature. Garnish with dollop of sour cream and chives, if desired.

Makes 4 to 6 servings

SHANGHAI SALAD

3 tablespoons vegetable oil
1 teaspoon minced fresh ginger
1 clove garlic, minced
1½ cups cooked flank steak or
    other meat, cut into ½-inch
    strips
1½ cups fresh *or* 1 package
    (6 ounces) frozen snow
    peas, thawed and drained
1 can (8 ounces) sliced water
    chestnuts, drained
½ cup green onions, cut into
    ½-inch pieces
2 tablespoons dry sherry
1 tablespoon soy sauce
½ teaspoon TABASCO® pepper
    sauce
Shredded lettuce

Heat oil in large skillet or wok. Add ginger and garlic; cook 1 minute. Add remaining ingredients except lettuce; stir-fry over high heat until heated through. Spoon onto bed of shredded lettuce. Serve hot with additional TABASCO sauce, if desired.   *Makes 3 to 4 servings*

PRAWNS-IN-SHELL

1 pound large raw prawns
2 tablespoons dry white wine,
    divided
½ teaspoon grated fresh
    gingerroot
¼ cup vegetable oil
2 tablespoons coarsely chopped
    green onions and tops
1 teaspoon coarsely chopped
    fresh gingerroot
1 clove garlic, chopped
2 small red chili peppers,*
    coarsely chopped
1 tablespoon sugar
3 tablespoons tomato ketchup
2 tablespoons KIKKOMAN® Soy
    Sauce
½ teaspoon cornstarch

Wash and devein prawns; do not peel. Cut prawns diagonally into halves; place in medium bowl. Sprinkle 1 tablespoon wine and grated ginger over prawns. Heat oil in hot wok or large skillet over high heat. Add prawns; stir-fry until completely pink or red. Add green onions, chopped ginger, garlic and chili peppers; stir-fry only until onions are tender. Combine sugar, ketchup, soy sauce, remaining 1 tablespoon wine and cornstarch; pour into pan. Cook and stir until sauce boils and thickens. Serve immediately. Garnish as desired.   *Makes 8 servings*

*Wear rubber gloves when working with chilies and wash hands in warm soapy water. Avoid touching face or eyes.

BEEF, PORK & LAMB

LEMONY BEEF, VEGETABLES & BARLEY

1 pound lean ground beef
8 ounces mushrooms, sliced
1 medium onion, chopped
1 clove garlic, crushed
1 can (14 ounces) ready-to-
    serve beef broth

½ cup quick-cooking barley
½ teaspoon salt
¼ teaspoon pepper
1 package (10 ounces) frozen
    peas and carrots, defrosted
1 teaspoon grated lemon peel

1. In large nonstick skillet, cook and stir ground beef, mushrooms, onion and garlic over medium heat 8 to 10 minutes or until beef is no longer pink, breaking beef up into ¾-inch crumbles. Pour off drippings.

2. Stir in broth, barley, salt and pepper. Bring to a boil; reduce heat to medium-low. Cover tightly; simmer 10 minutes.

3. Add peas and carrots; continue cooking 2 to 5 minutes or until barley is tender. Stir in lemon peel. *Makes 4 servings*

Favorite recipe from **National Cattlemen's Beef Association**

Lemony Beef, Vegetables & Barley

HUNAN STIR-FRY WITH TOFU

1 block tofu
½ pound ground pork
1 tablespoon dry sherry
1 teaspoon minced fresh
    gingerroot
1 clove garlic, minced
½ cup regular-strength chicken
    broth
1 tablespoon cornstarch

3 tablespoons KIKKOMAN® Soy
    Sauce
1 tablespoon vinegar
½ teaspoon crushed red pepper
1 tablespoon vegetable oil
1 onion, cut into ¾-inch pieces
1 green bell pepper, cut into
    ¾-inch pieces
Hot cooked rice

Cut tofu into ½-inch cubes; drain well on several layers of paper towels.
Meanwhile, combine pork, sherry, ginger and garlic in small bowl; let
stand 10 minutes. Blend broth, cornstarch, soy sauce, vinegar and red
pepper; set aside. Heat wok or large skillet over medium-high heat; add
pork. Cook, stirring to separate pork, about 3 minutes, or until lightly
browned; remove. Heat oil in same pan. Add onion and bell pepper; stir-
fry 4 minutes. Add pork and soy sauce mixture. Cook and stir until mixture
boils and thickens. Gently fold in tofu; heat through. Serve immediately
over rice.   *Makes 4 servings*

BEEF, PEPPERS AND TOMATO STIR-FRY

1 package (6.8 ounces) RICE-A-
    RONI® Beef Flavor
1 pound well-trimmed top
    sirloin steak
¼ cup margarine or butter,
    divided
    Salt and pepper (optional)
½ red or green bell pepper, cut
    into strips

½ yellow bell pepper, cut into
    strips
1 medium onion, sliced
4 plum tomatoes, sliced into
    quarters
2 tablespoons dry red wine
    or 1 tablespoon
    Worcestershire sauce

1. Prepare Rice-A-Roni® Mix as package directs.

2. While Rice-A-Roni® is simmering, thinly slice meat across the grain.

3. In second large skillet, melt 2 tablespoons margarine over medium-high
heat. Sauté meat 5 minutes or until no longer pink. Remove from skillet;
sprinkle with salt and pepper, if desired. Set aside; keep warm.

4. In same skillet, sauté peppers and onion in remaining 2 tablespoons
margarine 3 minutes or until crisp-tender. Stir in meat.

5. Meanwhile, add tomatoes and wine to rice during last 5 minutes of
cooking. Serve rice topped with meat mixture.   *Makes 4 servings*

Hot and Spicy Onion Beef

HOT AND SPICY ONION BEEF

2 tablespoons soy sauce,
    divided
1 tablespoon cornstarch,
    divided
¾ pound flank steak, thinly
    sliced across the grain
2 tablespoons dry sherry
1 teaspoon Oriental sesame oil
1 teaspoon chili paste
    (optional)

2 tablespoons vegetable oil
1 large onion (12 to
    14 ounces), sliced
    vertically
1 teaspoon minced garlic
    Dried whole red chili peppers
    to taste
1 tablespoon water

Combine 1 tablespoon soy sauce and 1 teaspoon cornstarch in medium
bowl. Add beef; stir to coat. Let stand 30 minutes. Combine remaining
tablespoon soy sauce, the sherry, sesame oil and chili paste in small bowl;
set aside. Heat wok or large skillet over high heat. Add vegetable oil,
swirling to coat sides. Add onion, garlic and chili peppers; cook and stir
until onion is tender. Add beef; stir-fry 2 minutes or until lightly browned.
Add soy sauce mixture and mix well. Combine remaining 2 teaspoons
cornstarch and the water; mix into onion mixture. Cook and stir until
sauce boils and thickens.   *Makes about 4 servings*

Favorite recipe from **National Onion Association**

MONGOLIAN LAMB

SESAME SAUCE

- 1 tablespoon sesame seeds
- ¼ cup soy sauce
- 1 tablespoon dry sherry
- 1 tablespoon red wine vinegar
- 1½ teaspoons sugar
- 1 clove garlic, minced
- 1 green onion with top, finely chopped
- ½ teaspoon Oriental sesame oil

LAMB

- 1 pound boneless lean lamb* (leg or shoulder)
- 2 small leeks, trimmed and thoroughly cleaned
- 4 green onions with tops
- 2 medium carrots, shredded
- 1 medium zucchini, shredded
- 1 green bell pepper, cut into matchstick pieces
- 1 red bell pepper, cut into matchstick pieces
- ½ small head napa cabbage, thinly sliced
- 1 cup bean sprouts
- 4 tablespoons vegetable oil, divided
- 4 slices peeled fresh ginger, divided
- Chili oil (optional)

For Sesame Sauce, place sesame seeds in small skillet. Carefully shake or stir over medium heat until seeds begin to pop and turn golden brown, about 2 minutes; cool. Crush seeds with mortar and pestle or place between paper towels and crush with rolling pin. Scrape up sesame paste with knife and transfer to small serving bowl. Add remaining sauce ingredients; mix well.

Slice meat across grain into 2×¼-inch strips. Cut leeks into 2-inch slivers. Repeat with green onions. Arrange meat and all vegetables on large platter. Have Sesame Sauce, vegetable oil, ginger and chili oil near cooking area.

Heat wok or electric griddle to 350°F. Cook one serving at a time. For each serving, heat 1 tablespoon vegetable oil. Add one slice ginger; cook and stir 30 seconds. Discard ginger. Add ½ cup meat strips; stir-fry until lightly browned, about 1 minute. Add 2 cups assorted vegetables; stir-fry 1 minute. Drizzle with 2 tablespoons Sesame Sauce; stir-fry 30 seconds. Season with a few drops chili oil. Repeat with remaining ingredients.

Makes 4 servings

*Or, substitute beef flank steak or boneless lean pork for the lamb.

Mongolian Lamb

SAVORY PORK & APPLE STIR–FRY

1 package (7.2 ounces) RICE-A-RONI® Rice Pilaf
1 ⅓ cups apple juice or apple cider, divided
1 pound boneless pork loin, pork tenderloin or skinless, boneless chicken breast halves
1 teaspoon paprika
1 teaspoon dried thyme leaves
½ teaspoon ground sage or poultry seasoning
½ teaspoon salt (optional)
2 tablespoons margarine or butter
2 medium apples, cored, sliced
1 teaspoon cornstarch
⅓ cup coarsely chopped walnuts

1. Prepare Rice-A-Roni® Mix as package directs, substituting 1 cup water and 1 cup apple juice for water in directions.

2. While Rice-A-Roni® is simmering, cut pork into 1½×¼-inch strips. Combine seasonings; toss with meat.

3. In second large skillet, melt margarine over medium heat. Stir-fry meat 3 to 4 minutes or just until pork is no longer pink.

4. Add apples; stir-fry 2 to 3 minutes or until apples are almost tender. Add combined remaining ⅓ cup apple juice and cornstarch. Stir-fry 1 to 2 minutes or until thickened to form glaze.

5. Stir in nuts. Serve rice topped with pork mixture.   *Makes 4 servings*

Savory Pork & Apple Stir-Fry

Oriental Beef & Noodle Toss

ORIENTAL BEEF & NOODLE TOSS

1 pound lean ground beef
2 packages (3 ounces each)
    Oriental flavor instant
    ramen noodles
2 cups water

2 cups frozen Oriental
    vegetable mixture
⅛ teaspoon ground ginger
2 tablespoons thinly sliced
    green onion

1. In large nonstick skillet, brown ground beef over medium heat 8 to 10 minutes or until beef is no longer pink, breaking up beef into ¾-inch crumbles. Remove with slotted spoon; pour off drippings. Season beef with one seasoning packet from noodles; set aside.

2. In same skillet, combine water, frozen vegetables, noodles (broken into several pieces), ginger and remaining seasoning packet. Bring to a boil; reduce heat. Cover; simmer 3 minutes or until noodles are tender, stirring occasionally.

3. Return beef to skillet; heat through. Stir in green onion before serving.

Makes 4 servings

Favorite recipe from **National Cattlemen's Beef Association**

STIR–FRY TOMATO BEEF

1 cup uncooked long-grain
  white rice
1 pound flank steak
1 tablespoon cornstarch
1 tablespoon soy sauce
2 cloves garlic, minced

1 teaspoon minced gingerroot
  or ¼ teaspoon ground
  ginger
1 tablespoon vegetable oil
1 can (14½ ounces)
  DEL MONTE® Original
  Recipe Stewed Tomatoes

1. Cook rice according to package directions.

2. Cut meat in half lengthwise, and then cut crosswise into thin slices.

3. In medium bowl, combine cornstarch, soy sauce, garlic and ginger. Add sliced meat; toss to coat.

4. Heat oil in large skillet over high heat. Add meat; cook, stirring constantly, until browned. Add tomatoes; cook until thickened, about 5 minutes, stirring frequently.

5. Serve over hot rice. Garnish with chopped cilantro or green onions, if desired.
Makes 4 to 6 servings

GINGER BEEF QUICK–FRY

1 can (8 ounces) DOLE® Chunk
  Pineapple in Juice
½ pound top sirloin steak
2 cloves garlic, pressed
½ teaspoon ground ginger
2 tablespoons vegetable oil
6 tablespoons pale dry sherry
3 tablespoons soy sauce

½ cup water
2 tablespoons cornstarch
1 bunch radishes, cut into
  halves
1 green bell pepper, seeded and
  chunked
1 cup sliced green onions
  Shredded lettuce

Drain pineapple, reserving juice. Cut steak into ½-inch-thick strips. Quickly cook and stir steak with garlic and ginger in hot oil. Combine reserved juice, sherry, soy sauce, water and cornstarch. Stir into beef mixture. Add pineapple, radishes, bell pepper and onions. Cook until sauce is clear and thickened. Serve over bed of shredded lettuce.
Makes 2 servings

Quick Trick: Beef is easier to slice when partially frozen. For best results use a serrated knife.

Stir-Fry Tomato Beef

GOLDEN PORK STIR–FRY

Sweet and Sour Cooking
Sauce (recipe follows)
2 tablespoons vegetable oil,
divided
1 clove garlic, crushed or finely
chopped
½ pound lean, boneless pork,
cut into thin strips
2 cups broccoli florets

1 sweet red or green bell
pepper, seeded and sliced
into thin strips
1 Golden Delicious apple,
cored and cut into 16 slices
4 cups sliced napa cabbage
Cooked rice or noodles
(optional)

1. Prepare Sweet and Sour Cooking Sauce; set aside. In large skillet or wok, heat 1 tablespoon oil over medium-high heat. Add garlic and stir-fry until lightly browned. Remove and discard garlic. Add pork to seasoned oil in skillet and stir-fry until browned; remove pork to bowl and reserve.

2. Add remaining tablespoon oil to skillet. Add broccoli and pepper; stir-fry about 1 minute. Add apple, cabbage, and reserved pork; stir-fry 2 minutes longer. Add Sweet and Sour Cooking Sauce and cook, stirring, until sauce thickens and coats all ingredients. Serve over rice or noodles.

Makes 4 servings

SWEET AND SOUR COOKING SAUCE: In small bowl, combine 2 tablespoons chicken broth or water, 1 tablespoon reduced-sodium soy sauce, 1 teaspoon cornstarch, 1 teaspoon sugar, 1 teaspoon grated fresh gingerroot, 1 teaspoon rice wine or cider vinegar, and ⅛ teaspoon crushed red pepper; stir until well-blended.

Favorite recipe from **Washington Apple Commission**

TERIYAKI BEEF

¾ pound sirloin tip steak, cut
into thin strips
½ cup teriyaki sauce
¼ cup water
1 tablespoon cornstarch

1 teaspoon sugar
1 bag (16 ounces) BIRDS EYE®
frozen Farm Fresh Mixtures
Broccoli, Carrots and
Water Chestnuts

• Spray large skillet with nonstick cooking spray; cook beef strips over medium-high heat 7 to 8 minutes, stirring occasionally.

• Combine teriyaki sauce, water, cornstarch and sugar; mix well.

• Add teriyaki sauce mixture and vegetables to beef. Bring to boil; quickly reduce heat to medium.

• Cook 7 to 10 minutes or until broccoli is heated through, stirring occasionally.

Makes 4 to 6 servings

BEEF & BROCCOLI PEPPER STEAK

1 tablespoon margarine or
    butter
1 pound well-trimmed top
    round steak, cut into thin
    strips

1 package (6.8 ounces) RICE-A-
    RONI® Beef Flavor
2 cups broccoli flowerets
½ cup red or green bell pepper
    strips
1 small onion, thinly sliced

1. In large skillet, melt margarine over medium heat. Add meat; sauté just until browned.

2. Remove from skillet; set aside. Keep warm.

3. In same skillet, prepare Rice-A-Roni® Mix as package directs; simmer 10 minutes. Add meat and remaining ingredients; simmer an additional 10 minutes or until most of liquid is absorbed and vegetables are crisp-tender.

Makes 4 servings

Beef & Broccoli Pepper Steak

SOUTHWESTERN LAMB STIR–FRY

12 ounces boneless lean
 American lamb, leg or
 shoulder, cut into ¼-inch
 strips
1 tablespoon vegetable oil
1 clove garlic, minced
1 large green bell pepper, cut
 into strips (about 1 cup)
1 medium onion, sliced and
 separated into rings (about
 1 cup)

2 tablespoons dry taco
 seasoning mix
1 cup coarsely chopped
 tomatoes
¼ cup green chili salsa
3 to 4 ounces baby corn ears,
 drained (optional)
1 cup lettuce, shredded
4 flour tortillas, warmed
 Optional toppings: shredded
 cheese, sliced black olives,
 sour cream, guacamole

Heat oil and garlic to medium-high in large wok or skillet. Stir in lamb
strips, bell pepper, onion rings and taco seasoning. Stir-fry 4 to 6 minutes
or until vegetables are crisp-tender and lamb is still slightly pink.

Add tomatoes, salsa and baby corn. Cook 1 to 2 minutes or until
thoroughly heated, stirring constantly. Place a layer of shredded lettuce
over warm tortilla. Top with lamb mixture and your choice of toppings.
Repeat with remaining tortillas.   *Makes 4 servings*

Favorite recipe from **American Lamb Council**

PORK WITH APPLES AND TOASTED WALNUTS

4 to 6 loin pork chops, about
 1 inch thick
 Salt and ground black pepper
2 tablespoons vegetable oil
1 clove garlic, minced
⅓ cup apple juice
1 cup (10-ounce jar) CROSSE &
 BLACKWELL® Ham Glaze

¾ teaspoon chopped fresh
 thyme *or* ¼ teaspoon dried
 thyme leaves
8 ounces (1 large or 2 small)
 tart green apples, sliced
¼ cup coarsely chopped
 walnuts, toasted

Season pork chops with salt and pepper. In large skillet, heat oil; brown
chops quickly on both sides. Remove from skillet and set aside.

Add garlic, apple juice, ham glaze, thyme and apples to skillet. Cook
2 minutes, stirring frequently. Return pork chops to skillet; simmer covered
5 to 6 minutes or until chops are tender. Stir in walnuts. Serve
immediately.   *Makes 4 to 6 servings*

Southwestern Lamb Stir-Fry

Beef & Vegetable Fried Rice

BEEF & VEGETABLE FRIED RICE

1 pound lean ground beef
2 cloves garlic, crushed
1 teaspoon grated fresh
  gingerroot *or* ¼ teaspoon
  ground ginger
2 tablespoons water
1 red bell pepper, cut into
  ½-inch pieces

1 package (6 ounces) frozen
  pea pods
3 cups cold cooked rice
3 tablespoons soy sauce
2 teaspoons dark sesame oil
¼ cup thinly sliced green onions

1. In large nonstick skillet, brown ground beef, garlic and ginger over medium heat 8 to 10 minutes or until beef is no longer pink, breaking beef up into ¾-inch crumbles. Remove with slotted spoon; pour off drippings.

2. In same skillet, heat water over medium-high heat until hot. Add bell pepper and pea pods; cook 3 minutes or until bell pepper is crisp-tender, stirring occasionally. Add rice, soy sauce and sesame oil; mix well. Return beef to skillet; heat through, about 5 minutes. Stir in green onions before serving. *Makes 4 servings*

Favorite recipe from **National Cattlemen's Beef Association**

SPICY–SWEET PINEAPPLE PORK

¾ cup LAWRY'S® Hawaiian
  Marinade with Tropical
  Fruit Juices
1 tablespoon minced fresh
  gingerroot
1 pound pork loin, cut into
  ½-inch strips or cubes
1 cup salsa
3 tablespoons brown sugar
2 tablespoons cornstarch

2 cans (8 ounces each)
  pineapple chunks, divided
2 tablespoons vegetable oil,
  divided
1 green bell pepper, cut into
  chunks
3 green onions, diagonally
  sliced into 1-inch pieces
½ cup whole cashews

In large resealable plastic bag, combine Hawaiian Marinade with Tropical Fruit Juices and the ginger. Add pork and marinate in refrigerator 1 hour. In small bowl, combine salsa, brown sugar, cornstarch and juice from one pineapple can; set aside. In large hot skillet or wok heat 1 tablespoon oil. Stir-fry bell pepper and onions until onions are transparent; remove and set aside. Add remaining 1 tablespoon oil and pork to skillet; stir-fry 5 minutes or until just browned. Return bell pepper and onions to skillet. Stir salsa mixture; add to skillet. Cook until thickened, stirring constantly. Drain remaining can of pineapple. Add pineapple chunks from both cans and cashews; simmer 5 minutes.   *Makes 6 servings*

BROCCOLI BEEF STIR–FRY

½ cup beef broth
4 tablespoons HOLLAND
  HOUSE® Sherry Cooking
  Wine, divided
1 tablespoon soy sauce
1 tablespoon cornstarch
1 teaspoon sugar
2 tablespoons vegetable oil,
  divided

2 cups fresh broccoli florets
1 cup fresh snow peas
1 red bell pepper, cut into strips
1 pound boneless top round or
  sirloin steak, slightly
  frozen, cut into thin strips
1 clove garlic, minced
  Hot cooked rice

To make sauce, in small bowl, combine broth, 2 tablespoons cooking wine, soy sauce, cornstarch and sugar; mix well. Set aside. In large skillet or wok, heat 1 tablespoon oil. Stir-fry broccoli, snow peas and bell pepper 1 minute. Add remaining 2 tablespoons cooking wine. Cover; cook 1 to 2 minutes. Remove from pan. Heat remaining 1 tablespoon oil; add meat and garlic. Stir-fry 5 minutes or until meat is browned. Add sauce to meat; cook 2 to 3 minutes or until thickened, stirring frequently. Add vegetables; cook until thoroughly heated. Serve over cooked rice.

Makes 4 servings

STIR–FRY OF WILD RICE, SNOW PEAS AND PORK

3 tablespoons vegetable oil
½ pound pork tenderloin, sliced ¼ inch thick
1 cup sliced celery
1 cup sliced green onions
1 cup sliced fresh mushrooms
1 can (8 ounces) sliced water chestnuts, drained
½ pound fresh or thawed frozen snow peas

1 tablespoon grated fresh gingerroot
2 cups cooked wild rice
3 tablespoons soy sauce
1 tablespoon dry sherry
½ teaspoon salt
1 tablespoon cornstarch
½ cup cashews, sunflower seeds or shredded or cut-out carrots for garnish

Heat oil in heavy skillet or wok; add pork and stir-fry over high heat for 2 minutes until meat is no longer pink. Add celery, green onions, mushrooms, water chestnuts, snow peas and ginger. Stir-fry for 5 minutes over high heat until vegetables are crisp-tender. Add wild rice, stirring until evenly blended. Combine soy sauce, sherry and salt; mix into cornstarch. Add to skillet, cooking and stirring about 1 minute until thickened and rice mixture is coated with glaze. Garnish, if desired.   *Makes 4 servings*

Favorite recipe from **Minnesota Cultivated Wild Rice Council**

GINGER BEEF & NOODLE STIR–FRY

1 pound flank steak, cut into thin strips
½ cup LAWRY'S® Thai Ginger Marinade with Lime Juice
1 tablespoon vegetable oil
2 cups broccoli florettes
1 red bell pepper, chopped
2 tablespoons soy sauce

1 teaspoon cornstarch
1 teaspoon LAWRY'S® Garlic Powder with Parsley
1 package (7 ounces) chuka soba noodles (Japanese-style noodles) prepared according to package directions

In large resealable plastic bag combine beef and Thai Ginger Marinade with Lime Juice; marinate in refrigerator 30 minutes. In large skillet, heat oil. Stir-fry broccoli and bell pepper over high heat 2 minutes; remove and set aside. In same skillet cook beef over high heat about 5 to 7 minutes. In small bowl combine soy sauce, cornstarch and Garlic Powder with Parsley; blend well. Add to beef; cook over medium heat until sauce is thickened. Stir in broccoli and bell pepper; heat through. Spoon over noodles.   *Makes 4 servings*

Hint: Vermicelli noodles may be substituted for chuka soba noodles.

Ma-Po Bean Curd

MA–PO BEAN CURD

1 tablespoon Szechuan peppercorns* (optional)	2 teaspoons minced fresh ginger
¾ cup chicken broth	12 to 14 ounces bean curd, drained and cut into ½-inch cubes
1 tablespoon soy sauce	
1 tablespoon dry sherry	
2 tablespoons vegetable oil	2 green onions, thinly sliced
4 ounces ground pork	3 tablespoons water
1 tablespoon hot bean sauce**	4½ teaspoons cornstarch
2 cloves garlic, minced	1 teaspoon Oriental sesame oil

Place peppercorns in small skillet; shake over medium-low heat, until fragrant, about 2 minutes. Let cool. Crush peppercorns with mortar and pestle or place between paper towels and crush with hammer; set aside.

Combine chicken broth, soy sauce and sherry in small bowl; set aside. Heat vegetable oil in wok or large skillet over high heat. Add pork and stir-fry until pork is no longer pink, about 2 minutes. Add hot bean sauce, garlic and ginger. Stir-fry until meat absorbs color from bean sauce, about 1 minute. Add chicken broth mixture and bean curd to wok. Simmer, uncovered, 5 minutes. Stir in onions. Blend water and cornstarch in small cup. Add to wok; cook and stir until sauce boils and thickens slightly. Stir in sesame oil. Pass crushed peppercorns to sprinkle over individual servings, if desired. *Makes 3 to 4 servings*

*Szechuan peppercorns are very potent. Wear rubber or plastic gloves when crushing them and do not touch eyes or lips when handling.

**Available in the Oriental section of large supermarkets or in specialty grocery stores.

POULTRY

CHICKEN AND VEGETABLES WITH MUSTARD SAUCE

1 tablespoon sugar
2 teaspoons cornstarch
1½ teaspoons dry mustard
2 tablespoons reduced-sodium soy sauce
2 tablespoons water
2 tablespoons rice vinegar
1 pound boneless skinless chicken breasts
4 teaspoons vegetable oil, divided

2 cloves garlic, minced
1 small red bell pepper, cut into short thin strips
½ cup thinly sliced celery
1 small onion, cut into thin wedges
3 cups hot cooked Chinese egg noodles (3 ounces uncooked)
Celery leaves for garnish

Combine sugar, cornstarch and mustard in small bowl. Blend soy sauce, water and vinegar into cornstarch mixture until smooth. Cut chicken into 1-inch pieces. Heat 2 teaspoons oil in wok or large nonstick skillet over medium heat. Add chicken and garlic; stir-fry 3 minutes or until chicken is no longer pink. Remove and reserve.

Add remaining 2 teaspoons oil to wok. Add bell pepper, celery and onion; stir-fry 3 minutes or until vegetables are crisp-tender. Stir soy sauce mixture; add to wok. Cook and stir 30 seconds or until sauce boils and thickens. Return chicken with any accumulated juices to wok; heat through. Serve over Chinese noodles. Garnish, if desired.

Makes 4 servings

Chicken and Vegetables with Mustard Sauce

Lemon Chicken Herb Stir-Fry

LEMON CHICKEN HERB STIR–FRY

4½ teaspoons peanut oil
2 green onions, cut into 1-inch pieces
1 large carrot, cut into ½-inch julienne
1 can (8 ounces) bamboo shoots
2 cups broccoli florets
1 pound boneless skinless chicken breast halves or boneless pork loin, sliced into strips

1 cup LAWRY'S® Herb & Garlic Marinade with Lemon Juice
1 tablespoon soy sauce
½ teaspoon arrowroot
1 can (11 ounces) mandarin orange segments, drained (optional)
1 tablespoon sesame seeds

In large wok or skillet, heat oil. Cook and stir onions and carrot 3 to 5 minutes until just tender. Stir in bamboo shoots, broccoli and chicken. Stir-fry 7 to 9 minutes until meat is just cooked. In small bowl, whisk together Herb & Garlic Marinade with Lemon Juice, soy sauce and arrowroot. Add to skillet; continue cooking, stirring constantly until sauce forms glaze on mixture. Stir in orange segments, if desired, and sprinkle with sesame seeds.

Makes 6 servings

TRADITIONAL FRIED RICE
WITH TURKEY AND PINE NUTS

1 bag SUCCESS® Brown Rice
1 tablespoon vegetable oil
1 medium green bell pepper,
   chopped
¼ pound fresh mushrooms,
   sliced

1 small onion, chopped
¼ pound chopped cooked
   turkey
¼ cup pine nuts, toasted
2 tablespoons reduced-sodium
   soy sauce (optional)

Prepare rice according to package directions. Rinse with cold water until rice is cool.

Heat oil in large skillet or wok over medium heat. Add bell pepper, mushrooms and onion; cook and stir until tender. Add rice, turkey, pine nuts and soy sauce; heat thoroughly, stirring occasionally.

Makes 6 servings

SHANTUNG CHICKEN

1 whole chicken breast,
   skinned and boned
2 tablespoons cornstarch,
   divided
3 tablespoons KIKKOMAN® Soy
   Sauce, divided
1 tablespoon dry sherry
1 clove garlic, minced
1 cup water
3 tablespoons vegetable oil,
   divided

½ pound fresh bean sprouts
¼ pound green onions and tops,
   cut into 1½-inch lengths,
   separating whites from tops
1 tablespoon slivered fresh
   gingerroot
1 tablespoon sesame seed,
   toasted
Hot cooked noodles

Cut chicken into narrow strips. Combine 1 tablespoon *each* cornstarch and soy sauce with sherry and garlic in small bowl; stir in chicken. Let stand 5 minutes. Meanwhile, blend water, remaining 1 tablespoon cornstarch and 2 tablespoons soy sauce; set aside. Heat 1 tablespoon oil in hot wok or large skillet over high heat. Add chicken and stir-fry 2 minutes; remove. Heat remaining 2 tablespoons oil in same pan; add bean sprouts, white parts of green onions and ginger; stir-fry 3 minutes. Stir in chicken, soy sauce mixture, green onion tops and sesame seed. Cook and stir until mixture boils and thickens. Serve immediately over noodles.

Makes 4 servings

SWEET 'N' SOUR CHICKEN STIR–FRY

3 tablespoons ketchup
1 tablespoon vinegar
1 tablespoon soy sauce
2 boneless skinless chicken breasts, cut into 1-inch cubes
1 tablespoon vegetable oil

½ package (16 ounces) frozen stir-fry vegetables or other frozen vegetable combination (such as broccoli, bell peppers, mushrooms and onions)
1 can (20 ounces) DOLE® Pineapple Chunks, drained

• **Combine** ketchup, vinegar and soy sauce in small bowl; set aside.

• **Cook** and stir chicken in large skillet or wok in hot oil over medium-high heat until chicken is browned.

• **Stir** in vegetables; cover. Reduce heat to low; cook 2 to 3 minutes or until vegetables are tender-crisp, stirring occasionally. Stir in pineapple and sauce; cook and stir until pineapple is heated through.

Makes 6 servings

Tip: Fresh vegetable combinations can be used in place of frozen vegetables. When using fresh vegetables, add 2 tablespoons of juice from canned pineapple and increase cooking time to 4 minutes or until vegetables are tender-crisp.

SIMPLE STIR–FRY CHICKEN

2 tablespoons vegetable oil
4 boneless skinless chicken breast halves, sliced into thin strips
1 green bell pepper, cut into 1-inch slivers
3 green onions, diagonally sliced into ½-inch pieces

1 package (10 ounces) frozen green peas
1 can (4 ounces) sliced mushrooms, drained
½ cup LAWRY'S® Stir-Fry Oriental Style Cooking Sauce

In wok or large skillet, heat oil. Stir-fry chicken strips in hot oil. When chicken is almost cooked, stir in bell pepper and onions; continue to stir-fry until vegetables are just tender yet colorful. Add peas, mushrooms and Stir-Fry Oriental Style Cooking Sauce; toss and cook until heated thoroughly. Serve over hot cooked rice.

Makes 4 servings

SANTA FE STIR–FRY

1 envelope LIPTON® Recipe
    Secrets® Onion Soup Mix*
¼ cup olive or vegetable oil
¼ cup water
1 tablespoon lime juice
    (optional)
½ teaspoon garlic powder

1 pound boneless skinless
    chicken breasts, cut into
    thin strips
2 cups frozen assorted
    vegetables, partially
    thawed and drained
Hot cooked rice

In 12-inch skillet, blend Onion Soup Mix, oil, water, lime juice and garlic powder; let stand 5 minutes. Bring to a boil over high heat; stir in chicken and vegetables. Cook uncovered, stirring frequently, 5 minutes or until chicken is done. Serve over hot rice. Garnish, if desired, with chopped fresh parsley and lime slices. *Makes about 4 servings*

*Also terrific with Lipton® Recipe Secrets® Onion-Mushroom or Savory Herb with Garlic Soup Mix.

LEMON TURKEY STIR–FRY

1 bunch green onions
½ pound medium-size
    mushrooms
1 small lemon
1 tablespoon Worcestershire
    sauce
2 teaspoons cornstarch
1 teaspoon honey
1 envelope chicken-flavored
    bouillon

1 package (16 ounces) turkey
    cutlets*
2 tablespoons vegetable oil
½ teaspoon LAWRY'S® Seasoned
    Salt
1 small zucchini, thinly sliced
1 small red bell pepper, thinly
    sliced

Cut green onions into 2-inch pieces; quarter mushrooms. Grate peel from lemon; place in small bowl. Squeeze juice into bowl. Stir in Worcestershire, cornstarch, honey, bouillon and ⅔ cup water. Cut turkey into ½-inch-wide strips. Heat oil in medium skillet; cook turkey with Seasoned Salt until turkey just loses its pink color, stirring constantly. Remove from skillet; set aside. In same skillet, cook zucchini, bell pepper, green onions and mushrooms until tender-crisp. Stir in cornstarch mixture. Cook, stirring until thickened. Add turkey; heat through.

Makes 4 servings

*1 pound cut-up cooked turkey can replace cutlets. Omit cooking stage of turkey and stir in at end to heat through.

Plum Chicken

PLUM CHICKEN

6 ounces fresh uncooked
   Chinese egg noodles
¼ cup plum preserves or jam
3 tablespoons rice wine vinegar
3 tablespoons reduced-sodium
   soy sauce
1 tablespoon cornstarch
3 teaspoons vegetable oil,
   divided

1 small red onion, thinly sliced
2 cups fresh snow peas,
   diagonally sliced into
   ½-inch pieces
12 ounces boneless skinless
   chicken breasts, cut into
   thin strips
4 medium plums or apricots,
   pitted and sliced

Cook noodles according to package directions, omitting salt. Drain and keep warm. Stir together plum preserves, vinegar, soy sauce and cornstarch in small bowl; set aside. Heat 2 teaspoons oil in large nonstick skillet or wok. Add onion and cook 2 minutes or until slightly softened. Add snow peas and cook 3 minutes. Remove mixture to bowl.

Heat remaining 1 teaspoon oil in skillet. Add chicken and cook over medium-high heat 2 to 3 minutes or until no longer pink. Push chicken to one side of skillet. Stir plum sauce; add to skillet. Cook and stir until thick and bubbly. Add vegetables and plums; stir to coat evenly. Cook 3 minutes or until heated through. Toss with noodles and serve immediately.

Makes 4 servings

ASPARAGUS CHICKEN WITH BLACK BEAN SAUCE

1 tablespoon dry sherry
4 teaspoons soy sauce, divided
5 teaspoons cornstarch, divided
1 teaspoon Oriental sesame oil
3 boneless skinless chicken
    breast halves, cut into
    bite-size pieces
1 tablespoon fermented, salted
    black beans*
1 teaspoon minced fresh ginger
1 clove garlic, minced

½ cup chicken broth
1 tablespoon oyster sauce
3 tablespoons vegetable oil,
    divided
1 pound fresh asparagus spears,
    trimmed and diagonally cut
    into 1-inch pieces
1 medium yellow onion, cut
    into 8 wedges and
    separated
2 tablespoons water

For marinade, combine sherry, 2 teaspoons soy sauce, 2 teaspoons cornstarch and the sesame oil in large bowl; mix well. Add chicken and stir to coat well. Let stand 30 minutes.

Place black beans in sieve and rinse under cold running water. Coarsely chop beans. Combine beans, ginger and garlic; finely chop all three together. Combine chicken broth, remaining 2 teaspoons soy sauce, the oyster sauce and remaining 3 teaspoons cornstarch in small bowl; mix well and set aside.

Heat 2 tablespoons vegetable oil in wok or large skillet over high heat. Add chicken and stir-fry about 3 minutes or until chicken is no longer pink. Remove and set aside. Heat remaining 1 tablespoon vegetable oil in wok. Add asparagus and onion; stir-fry 30 seconds. Add water; cover and cook, stirring occasionally, until asparagus is crisp-tender, about 2 minutes. Return chicken to wok. Stir chicken broth mixture and add to wok with bean mixture; cook and stir until sauce boils and thickens.

Makes 3 to 4 servings

*May be found in Oriental section of large supermarkets or specialty grocery stores.

Asparagus Chicken with Black Bean Sauce

CHICKEN CORN SAUTÉ

1 tablespoon chili powder
½ teaspoon salt
4 boneless, skinless chicken
    breast halves, cut into bite-
    size pieces (about 1 pound)
2 tablespoons CRISCO®
    Vegetable Oil, divided
1 cup chopped onion

2 medium green bell peppers,
    cut into strips
1 medium red bell pepper, cut
    into strips
1 package (10 ounces) frozen
    whole kernel corn, thawed
Hot pepper sauce (optional)

1. Combine chili powder and salt in shallow dish. Add chicken. Turn to coat.

2. Heat one tablespoon Crisco® Oil in large skillet on medium-high heat. Add chicken. Cook and stir until no longer pink in center. Remove to serving dish.

3. Heat remaining one tablespoon Crisco® Oil in skillet. Add onion. Cook and stir 2 minutes or until tender. Add bell peppers. Cook and stir 3 to 4 minutes or until crisp-tender. Add corn. Heat thoroughly, stirring occasionally. Return chicken to skillet to reheat. Season with hot pepper sauce, if desired.   *Makes 6 servings*

CHINESE CHICKEN & WALNUT STIR–FRY

¼ cup chicken broth or bouillon
2 tablespoons soy sauce
2 teaspoons cornstarch
2 teaspoons vegetable oil
¾ pound boneless skinless
    chicken breasts, cut into
    ¼-inch-thick strips
2 to 3 tablespoons slivered
    fresh ginger

1 clove garlic, minced
4 cups vegetables (snow peas,
    bean sprouts, very thinly
    sliced carrots and celery)
1 cup toasted walnut pieces
Hot cooked rice

Combine chicken broth, soy sauce and cornstarch; reserve. In wok or heavy skillet, heat oil until very hot but not smoking. Add chicken, ginger and garlic. Stir-fry over high heat 2 minutes; remove and reserve. Add vegetables to wok; toss until crisp-tender, 3 to 4 minutes. Return chicken to wok. Add cornstarch mixture; stir-fry 1 minute to thicken and coat. Add walnuts; toss. Serve immediately with rice.   *Makes 4 servings*
Favorite recipe from **Walnut Marketing Board**

Chicken Corn Sauté

CHICKEN CHOW MEIN

1 pound boneless skinless
   chicken breasts
2 cloves garlic, minced
1 package (6 ounces) frozen
   snow peas, thawed
1 teaspoon vegetable oil,
   divided
2 tablespoons reduced-sodium
   soy sauce

2 tablespoons dry sherry
3 large green onions, cut
   diagonally into 1-inch
   pieces
4 ounces uncooked Chinese egg
   noodles or vermicelli,
   cooked, drained and rinsed
1 teaspoon Oriental sesame oil

Cut chicken into 1-inch pieces. Toss with garlic in small bowl. Cut snow peas into halves. Heat ½ teaspoon vegetable oil in wok or large nonstick skillet over medium heat. Add chicken mixture; stir-fry 3 minutes or until chicken is no longer pink. Transfer to medium bowl; toss with soy sauce and sherry.

Heat remaining ½ teaspoon vegetable oil in wok. Add snow peas; stir-fry 1 minute. Add onions; stir-fry 30 seconds. Add chicken mixture; stir-fry 1 minute. Add noodles to wok; stir-fry 2 minutes or until heated through. Stir in sesame oil. Garnish, if desired.   *Makes 4 servings*

Chicken Chow Mein

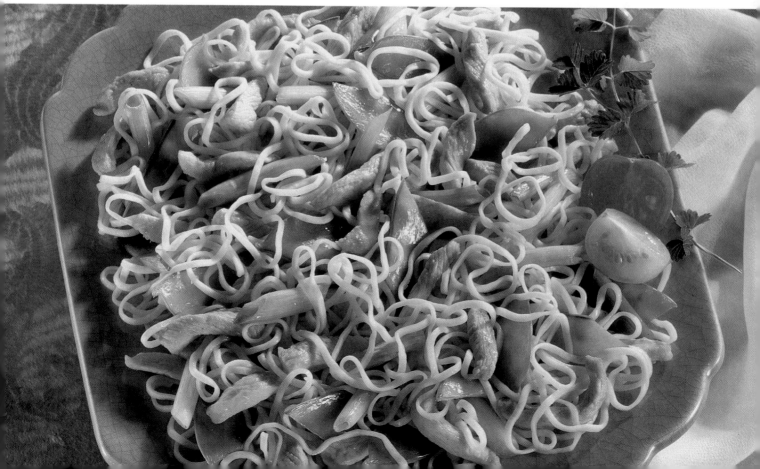

KAHLÚA® STIR–FRY CHICKEN

1½ pounds boneless skinless
    chicken, cut into ½-inch
    pieces
2 tablespoons beaten egg
¼ cup plus 2 tablespoons
    vegetable oil, divided
2 tablespoons plus 1 teaspoon
    cornstarch, divided
½ cup water chestnuts, sliced

6 asparagus tips, fresh or frozen
1 green bell pepper, cut into
    ½-inch strips
4 ounces mushrooms, sliced
4 ounces snow peas
3 tablespoons KAHLÚA®
1 cup cashews
3 green onions, chopped

Coat chicken in mixture of egg, 2 tablespoons oil and 2 tablespoons cornstarch. Heat remaining ¼ cup oil in wok or skillet. Add chicken. Cook until golden brown; remove and drain well. Remove all but 2 tablespoons oil from wok; heat. Add all vegetables except green onions. Stir-fry 3 to 5 minutes. Combine Kahlúa® and remaining 1 teaspoon cornstarch; add to vegetables. Bring to a boil, then simmer to slightly thicken. Add chicken and cashews; heat thoroughly. Remove to serving platter. Garnish with green onions.   *Makes 4 to 6 servings*

PEANUT CHICKEN STIR–FRY

1 package (6.1 ounces) RICE-A-
    RONI® With ⅓ Less Salt
    Fried Rice
½ cup reduced-sodium or
    regular chicken broth
2 tablespoons creamy peanut
    butter
1 tablespoon reduced-sodium
    or regular soy sauce
1 tablespoon vegetable oil

¾ pound skinless, boneless
    chicken breasts, cut into
    ½-inch pieces
2 cloves garlic, minced
2 cups frozen mixed carrots,
    broccoli and red bell
    pepper vegetable medley,
    thawed, drained
2 tablespoons chopped peanuts
    (optional)

1. Prepare Rice-A-Roni® Mix as package directs.

2. While Rice-A-Roni® is simmering, combine chicken broth, peanut butter and soy sauce; mix with a fork. Set aside.

3. In second large skillet or wok, heat oil over medium-high heat. Stir-fry chicken and garlic 2 minutes.

4. Add vegetables and broth mixture; stir-fry 5 to 7 minutes or until sauce has thickened. Serve over rice. Sprinkle with peanuts, if desired.

Makes 4 servings

SWEET 'N SOUR BROCCOLI CHICKEN

1 bunch DOLE® Broccoli
4 boneless skinless chicken
  breast halves
7 tablespoons cornstarch,
  divided
1 egg
1 teaspoon salt
Vegetable oil
1 can (8 ounces) DOLE®
  Pineapple Chunks in Juice
⅓ cup packed brown sugar

⅓ cup ketchup
¼ cup white vinegar
1 can (8 ounces) water
  chestnuts, drained, sliced
½ yellow onion, cut into ½-inch
  pieces, parboiled
½ DOLE® Red Bell Pepper, cut
  into ½-inch pieces
½ DOLE® Green Bell Pepper,
  cut into ½-inch pieces

• Cut broccoli into florets.

• Cut chicken into 2-inch pieces. Combine 6 tablespoons cornstarch, egg
and salt. Add chicken pieces and mix well to coat.

• In wok or large skillet, heat 2 cups oil to 375°F. Fry chicken (adding a
few pieces at a time) until crispy, about 3 minutes. Remove and drain all
but about 3 tablespoons oil. Stir-fry broccoli in remaining hot oil 1 minute.
Cover; steam 1 minute. Remove.

• Drain pineapple; reserve juice. Add enough water to juice to make 1½
cups liquid. Add to wok with brown sugar, ketchup, vinegar and
remaining 1 tablespoon cornstarch. Cook, stirring, until thickened.

• Add broccoli, chicken, pineapple, water chestnuts, onion and bell
peppers just before serving. Stir and cook to warm through.

Makes 6 servings

CANTON–STYLE FRIED RICE

1 package (6.2 ounces) RICE-A-
  RONI® Fried Rice
1 tablespoon vegetable oil
2 cups chopped cooked
  chicken, pork or shrimp

1 can (8 ounces) sliced water
  chestnuts or bamboo
  shoots, drained
1 egg, beaten
⅓ cup sliced green onions
Soy sauce (optional)

1. Prepare Rice-A-Roni® Mix as package directs.

2. In wok or large skillet, heat oil over medium heat. Add prepared Rice-
A-Roni®, chicken and water chestnuts. Stir-fry until heated through.

3. Stir in egg and onions; continue stirring until egg is cooked. Serve with
soy sauce, if desired.

Makes 4 servings

Shanghai Chicken with Asparagus and Ham

SHANGHAI CHICKEN
WITH ASPARAGUS AND HAM

**2 cups diagonally cut 1-inch
    asparagus pieces***
**1 pound boneless skinless
    chicken breasts**
2 teaspoons vegetable oil
¾ cup coarsely chopped onion

2 cloves garlic, minced
2 tablespoons teriyaki sauce
¼ cup diced deli ham
2 cups hot cooked white rice
**Carrot strips and fresh herbs
    for garnish**

To blanch asparagus pieces, cook 3 minutes in enough boiling water to cover. Plunge into cold water; drain well. Cut chicken into 1-inch pieces. Heat oil in large nonstick skillet over medium heat. Add onion and garlic; stir-fry 2 minutes. Add chicken; stir-fry 2 minutes. Add asparagus; stir-fry 2 minutes or until chicken is no longer pink. Add teriyaki sauce; mix well. Add ham; stir-fry until heated through. Serve over rice. Garnish, if desired.

Makes 4 servings

*Or substitute thawed frozen asparagus; omit blanching.

SWEET HONEY MUSTARD STIR–FRY WITH A KICK

4 boneless skinless chicken
   breast halves* (about
   1 pound), cut into ¼-inch
   strips
1 tablespoon vegetable oil
2 carrots, cut into ¼-inch
   julienne
1 medium onion, cut into
   wedges

¼ teaspoon LAWRY'S® Garlic
   Powder with Parsley
1 package (6 ounces) frozen
   Chinese pea pods
½ cup LAWRY'S® Dijon &
   Honey Barbecue Sauce
Dash of hot pepper sauce
Soy sauce to taste

In large skillet, cook and stir chicken in oil 5 minutes or until just browned. Remove; set aside. In same skillet, stir-fry carrots and onion with Garlic Powder with Parsley until tender-crisp. Return chicken to skillet; add pea pods, Dijon & Honey Barbecue Sauce and hot pepper sauce. Heat through. Sprinkle with soy sauce to taste.   *Makes 4 servings*

*1 pound lean pork butt cut into ¼-inch strips can replace chicken.

CHICKEN–CUCUMBER STIR FRY

2 whole broiler-fryer chicken
   breasts, halved, boned,
   skinned, cut into bite-size
   pieces
¼ cup water
¼ cup dry sherry
¼ cup soy sauce
2 tablespoons dark corn syrup
1 tablespoon vinegar
4 teaspoons cornstarch
¼ teaspoon crushed red pepper
⅛ teaspoon ground ginger

¼ cup vegetable oil
½ pound fresh mushrooms,
   sliced
1 bunch green onions, cut into
   2-inch pieces
1 can (8 ounces) water
   chestnuts, drained, sliced
2 cloves garlic, minced
1 cucumber, halved lengthwise,
   seeded, cut into thin 2-inch
   strips
12 cherry tomatoes, halved

In medium bowl, mix together water, sherry, soy sauce, corn syrup, vinegar, cornstarch, red pepper and ginger; set aside. Heat oil in wok or large skillet to medium-high. Add chicken; stir-fry 3 to 4 minutes or until chicken is lightly browned. Add mushrooms, green onions, water chestnuts and garlic; stir-fry 3 minutes. Add cucumber and stir-fry about 1 minute or until vegetables are crisp-tender. Add soy mixture and cook, stirring, until sauce thickens. Add cherry tomatoes and heat through.
       Makes 4 servings

Favorite recipe from **Delmarva Poultry Industry, Inc.**

CHICKEN FRIED RICE

1 bag SUCCESS® Rice
½ pound boneless skinless chicken, cut into ½-inch pieces
½ teaspoon salt
¼ teaspoon pepper
2 tablespoons vegetable oil
1 clove garlic, minced
½ teaspoon grated fresh ginger

2 cups diagonally sliced green onions
1 cup sliced fresh mushrooms
2 tablespoons reduced-sodium soy sauce
1 teaspoon sherry
1 teaspoon Asian-style hot chili sesame oil (optional)

Prepare rice according to package directions.

Sprinkle chicken with salt and pepper; set aside. Heat oil in large skillet over medium-high heat. Add garlic and ginger; cook and stir 1 minute. Add chicken; stir-fry until no longer pink in center. Add green onions and mushrooms; stir-fry until tender. Stir in soy sauce, sherry and sesame oil. Add rice; heat thoroughly, stirring occasionally. *Makes 6 servings*

Chicken Fried Rice

HOISIN CHICKEN

1 whole chicken (3 to
   4 pounds), cut up
½ cup plus 1 tablespoon
   cornstarch, divided
1 cup water
3 tablespoons dry sherry
3 tablespoons cider vinegar
3 tablespoons hoisin sauce
4 teaspoons soy sauce
2 teaspoons instant chicken
   bouillon granules
   Vegetable oil for frying
2 teaspoons minced fresh
   ginger

2 medium yellow onions,
   chopped
8 ounces fresh broccoli, cut
   into 1-inch pieces
1 red or green bell pepper,
   chopped
2 cans (4 ounces each) whole
   button mushrooms, drained
   Hot cooked vermicelli
   (optional)
   Additional red bell pepper,
   cut into strips, for garnish

Rinse chicken; set aside. Combine 1 tablespoon cornstarch, water, sherry, vinegar, hoisin sauce, soy sauce and bouillon granules in small bowl; mix well and set aside.

Place remaining ½ cup cornstarch in large bowl. Add chicken pieces; stir to coat well. Heat oil in large skillet or wok over high heat to 375°F. Add ⅓ of the chicken pieces, one piece at a time; cook until no longer pink in center, about 5 minutes. Drain chicken pieces on paper towels. Repeat with remaining chicken.

Remove all but 2 tablespoons oil from skillet. Add ginger; stir-fry 1 minute. Add onions; stir-fry 1 minute. Add broccoli, bell pepper and mushrooms; stir-fry 2 minutes. Stir cornstarch mixture; add to skillet. Cook and stir until sauce boils and turns translucent. Return chicken to skillet. Cook and stir until chicken is thoroughly heated, about 2 minutes. Serve over hot vermicelli and garnish with bell pepper strips, if desired.

Makes 6 servings

Hoisin Chicken

SEAFOOD

HOT AND SOUR SHRIMP

½ package (½ ounce) dried
    shiitake mushrooms*
½ small unpeeled cucumber
1 tablespoon brown sugar
2 teaspoons cornstarch
3 tablespoons rice vinegar
2 tablespoons reduced-sodium
    soy sauce
1 tablespoon vegetable oil

1 pound medium raw shrimp,
    peeled and deveined
2 cloves garlic, minced
¼ teaspoon crushed red pepper
    flakes
1 large red bell pepper, cut into
    short, thin strips
Hot cooked Chinese egg
    noodles (optional)

Place mushrooms in small bowl; cover with warm water. Soak 20 minutes
to soften. Drain; squeeze out excess water. Discard stems; slice caps. Cut
cucumber in half lengthwise; scrape out seeds. Slice crosswise. Combine
brown sugar and cornstarch in small bowl. Blend in vinegar and soy sauce
until smooth.

Heat oil in wok or large nonstick skillet over medium heat. Add shrimp,
garlic and crushed red pepper; stir-fry 1 minute. Add mushrooms and bell
pepper strips; stir-fry 2 minutes or until shrimp are opaque. Stir vinegar
mixture; add to wok. Cook and stir 30 seconds or until sauce boils and
thickens. Add cucumber; stir-fry until heated through. Serve over noodles,
if desired.
Makes 4 servings

*Or substitute ¾ cup sliced fresh mushrooms. Omit procedure for soaking mushrooms.

Hot and Sour Shrimp

THAI–STYLE TUNA FRIED RICE

4 to 5 tablespoons vegetable
oil, divided
2 eggs, lightly beaten
²/₃ cup raw medium shrimp,
peeled, chopped into
³/₄-inch pieces
3 cloves garlic, minced
1 to 2 tablespoons minced fresh
serrano chilies
4 to 6 cups cooked rice, chilled
overnight
1 tablespoon sugar

1 tablespoon nam pla (fish
sauce) (optional)
1 tablespoon soy sauce
1 can (6 ounces) STARKIST®
Solid White or Chunk Light
Tuna, drained and chunked
½ cup chopped dry-roasted
peanuts
¼ cup chopped fresh basil
2 tablespoons chopped fresh
cilantro
Lime wedges for garnish

In wok, heat 1 tablespoon oil over medium-high heat; add eggs and cook, stirring, until partially cooked but still runny. Return eggs to bowl. Wipe out wok with paper towels. Add 2 tablespoons oil to wok; heat.

Add shrimp, garlic and chilies. Stir-fry until shrimp turn pink, about 3 minutes. Remove shrimp mixture; set aside. Add remaining 1 or 2 tablespoons oil to wok; stir-fry rice, sugar, nam pla, if desired, and soy sauce until rice is heated through. Add tuna and peanuts; heat.

Return shrimp mixture and eggs to pan, chopping eggs into pieces with stir-fry spatula. Add basil and cilantro; toss gently to mix. Serve with lime wedges for garnish; squeeze juice on fried rice, if desired.

Makes 4 to 6 servings

Thai-Style Tuna Fried Rice

SCALLOPS WITH VEGETABLES

1 ounce dried mushrooms

2 tablespoons vegetable oil

2 yellow onions, cut into wedges and separated

3 stalks celery, diagonally cut into ½-inch pieces

8 ounces fresh green beans, trimmed and diagonally cut into 1-inch pieces

2 teaspoons minced fresh ginger

1 clove garlic, minced

1 cup water

2 tablespoons plus 1½ teaspoons dry sherry

4 teaspoons soy sauce

4 teaspoons cornstarch

2 teaspoons instant chicken bouillon granules

1 pound fresh or thawed frozen sea scallops, cut into quarters

6 green onions, diagonally cut into thin slices

1 can (15 ounces) baby corn, drained

Place mushrooms in bowl and cover with hot water. Let stand 30 minutes. Drain and squeeze out excess water. Discard stems; thinly slice caps. Heat oil in wok or large skillet over high heat. Add yellow onions, celery, green beans, ginger and garlic; stir-fry 3 minutes. Combine water, sherry, soy sauce, cornstarch and bouillon granules in small bowl. Add to wok; cook and stir until sauce boils. Add scallops, mushrooms, green onions and baby corn. Cook and stir until scallops turn opaque, about 4 minutes.

Makes 4 to 6 servings

SPICY TOFU AND SHRIMP

1 block firm tofu

1 tablespoon vegetable oil

½ pound shrimp, shelled and deveined

4 tablespoons LEE KUM KEE® Oyster Flavored Sauce, divided

1 teaspoon LEE KUM KEE® Chili Garlic Sauce

1 tablespoon water

1 green onion, chopped

1 teaspoon LEE KUM KEE® Sesame Oil

Drain tofu and cut into ¾-inch cubes. Set aside. Heat skillet or wok until hot; add vegetable oil and stir-fry shrimp with 2 tablespoons Lee Kum Kee® Oyster Flavored Sauce for about 1 minute or until shrimp just begin to turn opaque. Add tofu, remaining 2 tablespoons Lee Kum Kee® Oyster Flavored Sauce, the Lee Kum Kee® Chili Garlic Sauce and water. Gently stir, bringing sauce to a slow simmer. Sprinkle with chopped green onion and Lee Kum Kee® Sesame Oil; serve.

Makes about 4 servings

Scallops with Vegetables

FRAGRANT BRAISED OYSTERS

1 jar (10 or 12 ounces) shucked oysters, drained

2 cups plus 1 tablespoon water, divided

½ teaspoon salt

¼ cup chicken broth

1 tablespoon dry sherry

1 tablespoon oyster sauce

1 teaspoon cornstarch

¼ teaspoon sugar

2 tablespoons vegetable oil, divided

3 slices (about ½-inch each) pared fresh ginger, cut into thin slivers

½ small yellow onion, cut into wedges and separated

3 green onions, cut into 2-inch pieces

If oysters are large, cut into bite-size pieces. In 2-quart saucepan, bring 2 cups water and salt to a boil. Add oysters. Turn off heat and let stand 30 seconds. Drain, rinse under cold running water and drain again. Combine chicken broth, sherry, oyster sauce, remaining 1 tablespoon water, the cornstarch and sugar in small bowl; mix well. Heat 1 tablespoon oil in wok or large skillet over high heat. Add ginger and yellow onion; stir-fry 1 minute. Add green onions; stir-fry 30 seconds. Remove and set aside. Heat remaining 1 tablespoon oil in wok. Add blanched oysters and stir-fry 2 minutes. Return ginger and onions to wok. Stir cornstarch mixture and add to wok. Cook and stir until sauce boils and thickens.

Makes 2 to 3 servings

Fragrant Braised Oysters

Lemon-Garlic Shrimp

LEMON–GARLIC SHRIMP

1 package (6.2 ounces) RICE-A-RONI® With ⅓ Less Salt Broccoli Au Gratin
1 tablespoon margarine or butter
1 pound raw medium shrimp, shelled, deveined or large scallops, halved
1 medium red or green bell pepper, cut into short thin strips

2 cloves garlic, minced
½ teaspoon Italian seasoning
½ cup reduced-sodium or regular chicken broth
1 tablespoon lemon juice
1 tablespoon cornstarch
3 medium green onions, cut into ½-inch pieces
1 teaspoon grated lemon peel, divided

1. Prepare Rice-A-Roni® Mix as package directs.

2. While Rice-A-Roni® is simmering, heat margarine in second large skillet or wok over medium-high heat. Add shrimp, bell pepper, garlic and Italian seasoning. Stir-fry 3 to 4 minutes or until seafood is opaque.

3. Combine chicken broth, lemon juice and cornstarch, mixing until smooth. Add broth mixture and onions to skillet. Stir-fry 2 to 3 minutes or until sauce thickens.

4. Stir ½ teaspoon lemon peel into rice. Serve rice topped with shrimp mixture; sprinkle with remaining ½ teaspoon lemon peel.

Makes 4 servings

ALBACORE STIR–FRY

3 tablespoons vegetable oil
½ cup sliced onion
1 clove garlic, minced or
   pressed
1 bag (16 ounces) frozen
   Oriental vegetables,
   thawed and drained*

1 can (12 ounces) STARKIST®
   Solid White Tuna, drained
   and chunked
3 tablespoons soy sauce
1 tablespoon lemon juice
1 tablespoon water
1 teaspoon sugar
2 cups hot cooked rice

In wok or large skillet, heat oil over medium-high heat; cook and stir onion and garlic until onion is soft. Add thawed frozen vegetables; cook about 3 to 4 minutes or until crisp-tender. Add tuna, soy sauce, lemon juice, water and sugar. Cook 1 more minute; serve over rice.

Makes 4 servings

*May use 4 cups fresh vegetables such as carrots, snow peas, broccoli, bell peppers, mushrooms, celery and bean sprouts.

STIR–FRY SHRIMP AND CHICKEN

1 can (8 ounces) pineapple
   chunks
⅓ cup HEINZ® Chili Sauce
2 teaspoons cornstarch
2 teaspoons soy sauce
2 cups snow peas (about
   6 ounces)
1 cup diagonally sliced celery
8 to 10 green onions, cut into
   1-inch pieces

1 teaspoon minced gingerroot
2 tablespoons vegetable oil,
   divided
2 skinless boneless chicken
   breast halves, cut into
   1½-inch chunks
½ to ¾ pound deveined shelled
   large raw shrimp*

Drain pineapple, reserving juice; set pineapple aside. Combine reserved juice with chili sauce, cornstarch and soy sauce; set aside. In preheated wok or large skillet, stir-fry snow peas, celery, onions and gingerroot in 1 tablespoon oil 2 minutes or until tender-crisp; remove. Stir-fry chicken in remaining tablespoon oil 2 minutes; add shrimp and stir-fry 2 to 3 minutes longer. Return vegetables to wok; stir in reserved pineapple, then chili sauce mixture. Cook until sauce is thickened. *Makes 4 servings*

*1 package (12 ounces) shelled, deveined frozen shrimp, thawed, may be substituted.

Albacore Stir-Fry

SEAFOOD COMBINATION

Fried Noodles (recipe
   follows)
4 tablespoons vegetable oil,
   divided
8 green onions, diagonally cut
   into thin slices
3 stalks celery, diagonally cut
   into thin slices
1 can (8 ounces) water
   chestnuts, drained and cut
   into halves
1 can (8 ounces) bamboo
   shoots, thinly sliced
8 ounces fresh or thawed
   frozen sea scallops, cut into
   quarters

8 ounces fresh or thawed
   frozen shrimp, shelled and
   deveined
8 ounces fresh or thawed
   frozen fish fillets, skinned
   and cut into 1½-inch-
   square pieces
8 ounces cleaned, ready-to-
   cook squid (optional)
½ cup water
1 tablespoon soy sauce
2 teaspoons dry sherry
2 teaspoons cornstarch
1 teaspoon instant chicken
   bouillon granules

Prepare Fried Noodles; set aside. Heat 2 tablespoons oil in wok or large skillet over high heat. Add onions, celery, water chestnuts and bamboo shoots; stir-fry until crisp-tender, about 2 minutes. Remove and set aside.

Heat remaining 2 tablespoons oil in wok over high heat. Add scallops, shrimp, fish pieces and squid; stir-fry until all seafood turns opaque and is cooked through, about 3 minutes. Combine water, soy sauce, sherry, cornstarch and bouillon granules in small bowl. Add to wok. Cook and stir until liquid boils. Return vegetables to wok; cook and stir 2 minutes more. Serve with Fried Noodles. *Makes 6 servings*

FRIED NOODLES

8 ounces Chinese-style thin egg
   noodles

Vegetable oil for frying

Cook noodles according to package directions until tender but still firm, 2 to 3 minutes. Drain; rinse under cold running water and drain again. Place several layers of paper towels over cookie sheets or jelly-roll pans. Spread noodles over paper towels and let dry 2 to 3 hours. Heat oil in wok or large skillet over medium-high heat to 375°F. Using tongs or slotted spoon, lower a small portion of noodles into hot oil. Cook until golden, about 30 seconds. Drain on paper towels. Repeat with remaining noodles.

Garlic Shrimp with Wilted Spinach

GARLIC SHRIMP WITH WILTED SPINACH

2 teaspoons olive or vegetable
  oil
¼ cup diagonally sliced green
  onions
2 tablespoons sherry or dry
  white wine (optional)
1 envelope LIPTON® Recipe
  Secrets® Savory Herb with
  Garlic Soup Mix*

1 cup water
1 pound uncooked medium
  shrimp, peeled and
  deveined
1 large tomato, diced
2 cups fresh trimmed spinach
  leaves (about 4 ounces)
¼ cup chopped unsalted
  cashews (optional)

In 12-inch skillet, heat oil over medium heat and cook green onions,
stirring occasionally, 2 minutes or until slightly soft. Add sherry and bring
to a boil over high heat, stirring frequently. Stir in Savory Herb with Garlic
Soup Mix blended with water. Bring to a boil over high heat. Reduce heat
to low and simmer 2 minutes or until sauce is thickened. Stir in shrimp,
tomato, spinach and cashews. Simmer, stirring occasionally, 2 minutes or
until shrimp turn pink.   *Makes about 4 servings*

*Also terrific with Lipton® Recipe Secrets® Golden Herb with Lemon or Golden Onion
Soup Mix.

ORANGE ALMOND SCALLOPS

3 tablespoons fresh orange juice
1 tablespoon reduced-sodium soy sauce
1 clove garlic, minced
1 pound bay scallops or sea scallops, cut into halves
1 tablespoon cornstarch
1 teaspoon vegetable oil, divided
1 green bell pepper, cut into short, thin strips
1 can (8 ounces) sliced water chestnuts, drained and rinsed
3 tablespoons toasted blanched almonds
3 cups hot cooked white rice
½ teaspoon finely grated orange peel
Additional orange peel and fresh herbs for garnish

Combine orange juice, soy sauce and garlic in medium bowl. Add scallops; toss to coat. Marinate at room temperature 15 minutes or cover and refrigerate up to 1 hour. Drain scallops; reserve marinade. Blend marinade into cornstarch in small bowl until smooth. Heat ½ teaspoon oil in wok or large nonstick skillet over medium heat. Add scallops; stir-fry 2 minutes or until scallops are opaque. Remove and set aside. Add remaining ½ teaspoon oil to wok. Add bell pepper and water chestnuts; stir-fry 3 minutes. Return scallops along with any accumulated juices to wok. Stir marinade mixture and add to wok. Cook 1 minute or until sauce boils and thickens. Stir in almonds. Serve over rice. Sprinkle with grated orange peel. Garnish, if desired.   *Makes 4 servings*

SHRIMP FRIED RICE

2 eggs
2 tablespoons water
2 tablespoons vegetable oil
3 green onions and tops, chopped
3 cups cold, cooked rice
¼ pound cooked baby shrimp, chopped
3 tablespoons KIKKOMAN® Soy Sauce

Beat eggs with water just to blend; set aside. Heat oil in hot wok or large skillet over medium heat. Add green onions; stir-fry 30 seconds. Add eggs and scramble. Stir in rice and cook until heated, gently separating grains. Add shrimp and soy sauce; cook and stir until heated through. Serve immediately.   *Makes 6 servings*

Orange Almond Scallops

Seafood Stir-Fry with Indonesian Rice

SEAFOOD STIR–FRY WITH INDONESIAN RICE

2 cups water
1 cup long-grain rice
2 tablespoons reduced-sodium
  soy sauce
½ teaspoon red pepper flakes
¼ cup olive oil
½ cup chopped green onions
½ cup chopped celery
½ cup chopped green or red
  bell pepper
½ cup sliced mushrooms
1 cup broccoli, chopped
2 cups loosely packed spinach
  leaves or red cabbage

1 cup bean sprouts
2 cloves garlic, crushed
1 medium tomato, cut into
  wedges
12 ounces crab- or lobster-
  flavored surimi seafood,
  flake or chunk style
½ cup cucumber, sliced, for
  garnish
1 hard-boiled egg, chopped, for
  garnish
¼ cup dry-roasted peanuts, for
  garnish

Combine water, rice, soy sauce and red pepper flakes in 2-quart saucepan.
Cover and bring to a boil; reduce heat to low and cook 15 minutes, or
until rice is tender and water is absorbed, adding a little water if necessary.
Meanwhile, heat oil in wok or 12-inch skillet. Add onions, celery, bell
pepper and mushrooms and cook 3 minutes. Add broccoli and cook
2 minutes. Stir in spinach, bean sprouts and garlic; add cooked rice.
Reduce heat to low; arrange tomato and surimi seafood over mixture.
Cover and cook until heated through, about 3 minutes. Garnish with
cucumber, egg and peanuts, if desired.   *Makes 6 servings*

Favorite recipe from **Surimi Seafood Education Center**

SZECHUAN SHRIMP & PASTA

8 ounces linguine
1 pound medium shrimp, peeled and deveined
2 teaspoons MCCORMICK® Szechuan Style Pepper Blend, divided
2 tablespoons vegetable oil, divided
¼ teaspoon MCCORMICK® Garlic Powder

½ teaspoon MCCORMICK® Ground Ginger
1 red bell pepper, sliced into strips
8 ounces fresh snow peas or sugar snap peas
¾ cup water
¼ cup soy sauce
2 teaspoons cornstarch

1. Cook linguine according to package directions.

2. Sprinkle shrimp with 1 teaspoon Szechuan Style Pepper Blend. Heat 1 tablespoon oil in 10-inch skillet over medium-high heat. Add shrimp; sprinkle with Garlic Powder and Ginger. Stir-fry 3 minutes or until shrimp are pink. Remove and set aside.

3. Add remaining 1 tablespoon oil to skillet. Stir-fry pepper strips and snow peas 2 minutes or until vegetables are tender. Combine water, soy sauce, cornstarch and remaining 1 teaspoon Szechuan Style Pepper Blend. Add to vegetables in skillet; cook 1 to 2 minutes or until thickened, stirring occasionally. Return shrimp to skillet; heat through. Serve over linguine.

Makes 4 servings

PENNE WITH ASPARAGUS AND SHRIMP

1 envelope GOOD SEASONS® Garlic & Herb Salad Dressing Mix
6 asparagus spears, cut into 1-inch pieces
½ pound medium shrimp, cleaned

1 small red pepper, cut into thin strips
8 ounces penne or ziti pasta
1 package (4 ounces) ATHENOS® Natural Crumbled Feta Cheese

PREPARE salad dressing mix as directed on envelope.

HEAT 1 tablespoon of prepared dressing in large nonstick skillet on medium heat. Add asparagus; cook and stir 3 minutes. Add shrimp and red pepper; cover. Cook 5 minutes or until shrimp are pink and vegetables are tender-crisp, stirring occasionally.

MEANWHILE, cook pasta as directed on package; drain. Place in large serving bowl. Toss with remaining dressing, shrimp mixture and cheese. Serve immediately or refrigerate and serve chilled. *Makes 6 servings*

HALIBUT WITH CILANTRO AND LIME

1 pound halibut, tuna or
   swordfish steaks
2 tablespoons fresh lime juice
¼ cup reduced-sodium soy
   sauce
1 teaspoon cornstarch
½ teaspoon minced fresh ginger

½ teaspoon vegetable oil
½ cup slivered red or yellow
   onion
2 cloves garlic, minced
¼ cup coarsely chopped
   cilantro
Lime wedges for garnish

Cut halibut into 1-inch pieces; sprinkle with lime juice. Blend soy sauce into cornstarch in cup until smooth. Stir in ginger. Heat oil in wok or large nonstick skillet over medium heat. Add onion and garlic; stir-fry 2 minutes. Add halibut; stir-fry 2 minutes or until halibut is opaque. Stir soy sauce mixture; add to wok. Stir-fry 30 seconds or until sauce boils and thickens. Sprinkle with cilantro. Garnish, if desired.   *Makes 4 servings*

TASTY THAI SHRIMP & SESAME NOODLES

1 pound medium shrimp,
   shelled and deveined
1 (8-ounce) bottle NEWMAN'S
   OWN® Light Italian
   Dressing, divided
2 tablespoons chunky peanut
   butter
1 tablespoon soy sauce
1 tablespoon honey
1 teaspoon grated peeled
   gingerroot

½ teaspoon crushed red pepper
8 ounces capellini or angel hair
   pasta, uncooked
2 tablespoons vegetable oil
1 tablespoon Oriental sesame
   oil
1 medium carrot, peeled and
   shredded
1 cup chopped green onions
¼ cup chopped fresh cilantro
   for garnish

In medium bowl, combine shrimp with ⅓ cup Newman's Own® Light Italian Dressing. Cover and refrigerate 1 hour. In small bowl, with wire whisk or fork, mix peanut butter, soy sauce, honey, ginger, crushed red pepper and remaining dressing; set aside. Prepare capellini as label directs; drain.

Meanwhile, in 4-quart saucepan over high heat, heat vegetable and sesame oils until very hot. Add carrot and cook 1 minute. Drain shrimp; discard dressing. Add shrimp and green onions to carrot and cook, stirring constantly, approximately 3 minutes or until shrimp turn opaque. In large bowl, toss hot capellini with peanut butter and shrimp mixtures. Sprinkle with chopped cilantro, if desired.   *Makes 4 servings*

Halibut with Cilantro and Lime

VEGETABLES & MORE

MOO SHU VEGETABLES

½ package dried shiitake
    mushrooms (6 to
    7 mushrooms)
2 tablespoons peanut or
    vegetable oil
2 cloves garlic, minced
2 cups shredded napa cabbage,
    shredded green cabbage,
    preshredded cabbage or
    coleslaw mix
1 red bell pepper, cut into
    short, thin strips

1 cup fresh or rinsed and
    drained canned bean
    sprouts
2 large green onions, cut into
    short, thin strips
¼ cup hoisin sauce
⅓ cup plum sauce
8 (6- to 7-inch) flour tortillas,
    warmed

Place mushrooms in small bowl; cover with warm water. Soak 20 minutes to soften. Drain, squeezing out excess water. Discard mushroom stems; slice caps. Heat wok or large skillet over medium-high heat. Add oil; heat until hot. Add garlic; stir-fry 30 seconds. Stir in cabbage, mushrooms and bell pepper; stir-fry 3 minutes. Add bean sprouts and onions; stir-fry 2 minutes. Add hoisin sauce; stir-fry 30 seconds or until mixture is hot.

Spread about 2 teaspoons plum sauce down center of each tortilla. Spoon heaping ¼ cup vegetable mixture over sauce. Fold bottom of tortilla up over filling and fold sides over filling to form bundle.   *Makes 8 servings*

Moo Shu Vegetables

MUSTARD STIR–FRY

2 tablespoons vegetable oil
1 cup chopped broccoli
1 cup thinly sliced red bell
   pepper

4 tablespoons LAWRY'S®
   Dijon-Honey Barbecue
   Sauce

In skillet or wok heat oil. Add broccoli and bell pepper; cook and stir 2 to
3 minutes. Add Dijon-Honey Barbecue Sauce and simmer 3 minutes.

Makes 4 servings

SWEET AND SOUR STIR–FRY PASTA

2 cups vegetable-flavored pasta
2 cups water, divided
¼ cup cornstarch
½ cup pineapple juice
¼ cup cooking sherry
¼ cup soy sauce
2 tablespoons chicken-flavored
   instant bouillon
1 clove garlic, minced
3 tablespoons vegetable oil
1 cup chopped onion
1 cup chopped celery

1 cup yellow beans, cut into
   ½-inch pieces
1 cup baby corn chunks
¾ cup peeled, seeded ½-inch
   cucumber pieces
¾ cup zucchini, sliced
½ cup green bell pepper pieces
   (about ½ inch long)
½ cup sweet red bell pepper
   pieces (about ½ inch long)
¾ cup pineapple chunks

Cook pasta according to package directions; drain and set aside.

Mix ½ cup water with cornstarch. In 2-quart saucepan, mix remaining 1½
cups water, pineapple juice, sherry, soy sauce, chicken bouillon and
garlic. Bring to a boil over low heat, stirring frequently. Add cornstarch
mixture and boil until clear. Remove from heat and set aside, keeping
warm.

In wok or large skillet heat oil over medium heat; add onion and stir-fry
until transparent. Add remaining ingredients except pineapple chunks and
stir-fry until crisp-tender. Add sauce and cook 5 minutes. Add pineapple
chunks and pasta; cook over low heat until heated through.

Makes 6 to 8 servings

Favorite recipe from **North Dakota Wheat Commission**

Vegetable Fried Rice

VEGETABLE FRIED RICE

1 teaspoon vegetable oil
1½ cups small broccoli florets
½ cup chopped red bell pepper
2 cups chilled cooked white
    rice

1 tablespoon reduced-sodium
    soy sauce
½ cup shredded carrot

Heat oil in large nonstick skillet over medium heat. Add broccoli and bell pepper; stir-fry 3 minutes or until crisp-tender. Add rice and soy sauce; stir-fry 2 minutes. Add carrot; heat through. *Makes 4 servings*

CHEESY VEGETARIAN STIR–FRY

2 teaspoons olive oil
3 cloves garlic, minced
1 cup thinly sliced onion
4 cups small zucchini squash,
    cut lengthwise in quarters
    then into 1½-inch pieces
1 to 2 teaspoons dried Italian
    herbs

1 (9-ounce) package frozen
    artichoke hearts, thawed,
    cooked and drained
    (optional)
½ cup marinara sauce
½ cup shredded JARLSBERG
    Lite™ Cheese

Heat oil in wok over high heat; stir-fry garlic and onion 3 minutes or until lightly browned. Add zucchini and herbs; stir-fry 3 minutes or until crisp-tender. Remove from heat and stir in artichoke hearts, marinara sauce and Jarlsberg Lite™.

Serve with cannellini beans or over pasta such as orrechiette or linguine.

Makes 4 to 6 servings

HOT & SPICY GLAZED CARROTS

2 tablespoons vegetable oil
2 dried whole red chili peppers
1 pound carrots, peeled and cut
    diagonally into ⅛-inch
    slices

¼ cup KIKKOMAN® Teriyaki
Baste & Glaze

Heat oil in hot wok or large skillet over high heat. Add chili peppers and stir-fry until darkened; remove and discard. Add carrots; reduce heat to medium. Stir-fry 4 minutes, or until tender-crisp. Stir in teriyaki baste & glaze and cook until carrots are glazed. Garnish as desired. Serve immediately.

Makes 4 servings

DRAGON TOFU

¼ cup soy sauce
1 tablespoon creamy peanut
    butter
1 package (about 12 ounces)
    firm tofu, drained
1 medium zucchini
1 medium yellow squash
2 teaspoons peanut or
    vegetable oil

½ teaspoon hot chili oil
2 cloves garlic, minced
2 cups (packed) torn fresh
    spinach leaves
¼ cup coarsely chopped
    cashews or peanuts
    (optional)

Whisk soy sauce into peanut butter in small bowl. Press tofu lightly between paper towels; cut into ¾-inch squares or triangles. Place in single layer in shallow dish. Pour soy sauce mixture over tofu; stir gently to coat all surfaces. Let stand at room temperature 20 minutes. Cut zucchini and yellow squash lengthwise into ¼-inch-thick slices; cut each slice into 2×¼-inch strips. Heat nonstick skillet over medium-high heat. Add peanut and chili oils; heat until hot. Add garlic, zucchini and yellow squash; stir-fry 3 minutes. Add tofu mixture; cook 2 minutes or until tofu is heated through and sauce is slightly thickened, stirring occasionally. Stir in spinach; remove from heat. Sprinkle with cashews, if desired.

Makes 2 servings

Dragon Tofu

BROCCOLI & RED PEPPER SAUTÉ

2 tablespoons olive or
    vegetable oil
4 cups small broccoli florets
1 large red bell pepper, cut into
    thin strips
1 medium onion, sliced
1 clove garlic, finely chopped

1 envelope LIPTON® Recipe
    Secrets® Golden Herb with
    Lemon Soup Mix*
1 cup water
¼ cup sliced almonds, toasted
    (optional)

In 12-inch skillet, heat oil over medium heat and cook broccoli, bell pepper, onion and garlic 5 minutes or until onion is tender, stirring occasionally. Combine Golden Herb with Lemon Soup Mix with water; add to vegetable mixture. Simmer covered 5 minutes or until broccoli is tender. Sprinkle with almonds. *Makes about 6 servings*

*Also terrific with Lipton® Recipe Secrets® Savory Herb with Garlic Soup Mix.

BEAN CURD WITH OYSTER SAUCE

2 tablespoons vegetable oil,
    divided
8 ounces tofu, cut into ½-inch
    cubes
½ cup water
2 tablespoons oyster sauce
4 teaspoons dry sherry
4 teaspoons soy sauce
1 tablespoon cornstarch

4 ounces fresh mushrooms,
    sliced
6 green onions, cut into 1-inch
    pieces
3 stalks celery, diagonally cut
    into ½-inch pieces
1 red or green bell pepper, cut
    into ½-inch chunks

Heat 1 tablespoon oil in wok or large skillet over high heat. Add tofu and stir-fry until light brown, about 3 minutes. Remove and set aside. Combine water, oyster sauce, sherry, soy sauce and cornstarch in small bowl. Heat remaining 1 tablespoon oil in wok over high heat. Add remaining ingredients; stir-fry 1 minute. Return tofu to wok; toss lightly to combine. Add oyster sauce mixture to wok. Cook and stir until liquid boils; cook 1 minute more. *Makes 4 servings*

Broccoli & Red Pepper Sauté

HOT AND SPICY SPINACH

1 red bell pepper, cut into
    1-inch pieces
1 clove garlic, minced
1 pound prewashed fresh
    spinach, rinsed and
    chopped

1 tablespoon prepared mustard
1 teaspoon lemon juice
¼ teaspoon red pepper flakes

Spray large skillet with nonstick cooking spray; heat over medium heat. Add bell pepper and garlic; cook and stir 3 minutes. Add spinach; cook and stir 3 minutes or just until spinach begins to wilt. Stir in mustard, lemon juice and red pepper flakes. Serve immediately.

Makes 4 servings

Hot and Spicy Spinach

VEGETARIAN TOFU STIR–FRY

1 block tofu
2 tablespoons vegetable oil
1 teaspoon minced fresh
    gingerroot
1 medium onion, chunked
⅛ teaspoon salt
6 ounces fresh snow peas,
    trimmed and cut diagonally
    in half

⅓ cup KIKKOMAN® Stir-Fry
    Sauce
2 medium-size fresh tomatoes,
    chunked
¼ cup slivered blanched
    almonds, toasted

Cut tofu into ½-inch cubes; drain well on several layers of paper towels. Heat oil in hot wok or large skillet over high heat. Add ginger; stir-fry 30 seconds or until fragrant. Add onion and salt; stir-fry 2 minutes. Add snow peas; stir-fry 1 minute. Add stir-fry sauce, tomatoes and tofu. Gently stir to coat tofu and vegetables with sauce. Reduce heat and cook only until tomatoes and tofu are heated through. Sprinkle with almonds; serve immediately.
Makes 4 servings

STIR–FRY VEGETABLES

1 cup GRANDMA'S® Robust
    Flavor Molasses
¼ cup chicken broth
4 teaspoons cornstarch
2 tablespoons soy sauce
1 tablespoon minced garlic
1 tablespoon minced fresh
    ginger

⅛ teaspoon ground red pepper
1 tablespoon canola oil
2 pounds fresh vegetables
    sliced into bite-size pieces
    (celery, zucchini, onion,
    bell peppers, Chinese
    cabbage and snow peas)

Combine Grandma's® Molasses, broth, cornstarch, soy sauce, garlic, ginger, and ground red pepper. Set aside. Heat oil in wok or large heavy skillet. Add vegetables and stir-fry 2 to 3 minutes or until crisp-tender. Mix in molasses mixture. Cook just until sauce thickens and coats vegetables.
Makes 4 to 6 servings

Eggplant Szechuan Style

EGGPLANT SZECHUAN STYLE

1 pound Oriental eggplants *or*
    1 domestic eggplant
3 green onions, divided
1 tablespoon minced garlic
2 teaspoons minced fresh
    ginger
2 teaspoons hot bean sauce
½ cup chicken broth

1 tablespoon soy sauce
1 tablespoon red wine vinegar
1½ teaspoons sugar
5 tablespoons vegetable oil,
    divided
1 tablespoon water
1 teaspoon cornstarch
1 teaspoon Oriental sesame oil

Cut unpeeled eggplants into ½-inch-thick slices; cut slices into 2×½-inch
strips. Cut 1 onion into thin slices; reserve for garnish. Cut remaining
onions into thin slices; combine onions, garlic, ginger and hot bean sauce
in medium bowl. Combine chicken broth, soy sauce, vinegar and sugar in
small bowl.

Heat 2 tablespoons vegetable oil in wok or large skillet over medium-high
heat. Add ½ of eggplant and cook, stirring often, until soft and moist,
about 5 minutes. Remove to colander; drain. Repeat, using 2 more
tablespoons vegetable oil and remaining eggplant.

Heat remaining 1 tablespoon vegetable oil in wok over medium-high heat
until hot. Add onion-garlic mixture and stir-fry 30 seconds; return eggplant
to wok. Add chicken broth mixture. Bring to a boil and cook, stirring
occasionally, until liquid is almost evaporated. Blend water and cornstarch
in small cup; add to wok. Cook and stir until sauce boils and thickens
slightly. Stir in sesame oil. Garnish with reserved onion slices.

Makes 4 to 5 servings

FRESH VEGETABLE SAUTÉ

2 tablespoons olive oil
6 cups assorted cut-up
   vegetables, such as
   broccoli flowerets, green
   beans, cauliflowerets, sugar
   snap peas, bell pepper
   strips, diagonally sliced
   carrots, mushrooms,
   onions, yellow squash and
   zucchini

1 envelope GOOD SEASONS®
   Italian Salad Dressing Mix
2 tablespoons red wine vinegar

HEAT oil in large skillet on medium-high heat. Add vegetables; cook and stir until tender-crisp.

ADD salad dressing mix and vinegar; cook and stir until heated through. Garnish with chopped fresh parsley, if desired.   *Makes 4 to 6 servings*

Fresh Vegetable Sauté

VEGETABLE LO MEIN

8 ounces uncooked vermicelli
    or thin spaghetti, cooked
    and drained
¾ teaspoon Oriental sesame oil
½ teaspoon vegetable oil
3 cloves garlic, minced
1 teaspoon grated fresh ginger
2 cups sliced bok choy
½ cup sliced green onions
2 cups shredded carrots

6 ounces firm tofu, drained and
    cubed
6 tablespoons rice wine vinegar
¼ cup plum preserves
¼ cup water
1 teaspoon reduced-sodium soy
    sauce
½ teaspoon crushed red pepper
    flakes

Toss vermicelli with sesame oil in large bowl until well coated. Heat vegetable oil in large nonstick skillet or wok over medium heat. Stir in garlic and ginger; stir-fry 10 seconds. Add bok choy and onions; stir-fry 3 to 4 minutes until crisp-tender. Add carrots and tofu; stir-fry 2 to 3 minutes until carrots are crisp-tender.

Combine vinegar, preserves, water, soy sauce and crushed red pepper in small saucepan. Heat over medium heat until preserves are melted, stirring constantly. Combine noodles, vegetable mixture and sauce in large bowl; mix well.

Makes 6 servings

HOT AND SPICY VEGETABLE STIR–FRY

3 tablespoons CRISCO® Savory
    Seasonings Hot & Spicy
    Flavor oil
4 cups broccoli florets
1 red bell pepper, ribs and
    seeds removed, thinly
    sliced

1 yellow bell pepper, ribs and
    seeds removed, thinly
    sliced
1 medium onion, thinly sliced
1 tablespoon soy sauce
1 teaspoon salt or to taste

• **Heat** oil in heavy skillet or wok until very hot.

• **Add** broccoli, sliced red and yellow peppers and onion. **Toss** frequently, until tender but still crisp, about 5 minutes.

• **Add** soy sauce and salt. **Cook** 1 minute more. **Serve** immediately.

Makes 6 servings

Vegetable Lo Mein

PINEAPPLE VEGETABLE STIR–FRY

1 medium DOLE® Fresh
    Pineapple
1 cup red onion chunks
½ cup reduced-sodium chicken
    broth
1 tablespoon sherry
1 large clove garlic, pressed

¼ pound snow peas, trimmed,
    cut into thirds
1 tablespoon soy sauce
1 teaspoon Oriental sesame oil
½ cup halved cherry tomatoes
2 tablespoons chopped cilantro

• Twist crown from pineapple. Cut pineapple lengthwise in half. Reserve ½ for another use. Cut remaining half again lengthwise. Cut fruit from shells and trim off core. Cut fruit into chunks.

• In large skillet or wok cook onion in chicken broth over medium-high heat 4 minutes. Add sherry and garlic; cook 1 minute longer, stirring. Add pineapple; stir-fry 2 minutes. Add snow peas, soy sauce and sesame oil; stir-fry 1 minute. Remove from heat; stir in cherry tomatoes and cilantro.

Makes 4 servings

SESAME BROCCOLI STIR–FRY

1 tablespoon soy sauce
2 teaspoons cornstarch
⅓ cup HEINZ® Chili Sauce
¼ teaspoon Oriental sesame oil
1 tablespoon vegetable oil
4 cups broccoli florets
1 small red bell pepper, cut into
    strips (about ½ cup)

1 cup quartered small fresh
    mushrooms
1 small onion, cut into thin
    wedges
2 teaspoons toasted sesame
    seeds

In small bowl, combine soy sauce and cornstarch. Stir in chili sauce and sesame oil; set aside. In large skillet or wok, heat vegetable oil over medium-high heat until hot. Stir-fry broccoli and bell pepper 1 minute. Add mushrooms and onion; stir-fry 1 minute. Stir in chili sauce mixture; heat, stirring, until sauce is thickened and vegetables are coated. Sprinkle with sesame seeds before serving.

Makes 4 servings

Confetti Rice Pilaf

CONFETTI RICE PILAF

1 tablespoon margarine or
    butter
1 cup regular or converted rice
1 cup fresh or drained canned
    sliced mushrooms

2 medium carrots, diced
1 envelope LIPTON® Recipe
    Secrets® Savory Herb with
    Garlic Soup Mix*
2¼ cups water

In 12-inch skillet, melt margarine over medium-high heat and cook rice, stirring frequently, until golden. Stir in mushrooms, carrots and Savory Herb with Garlic Soup Mix blended with water. Bring to a boil over high heat. Reduce heat to low and simmer covered 20 minutes or until rice is tender.   *Makes about 6 servings*

*Also terrific with Lipton® Recipe Secrets® Golden Herb with Lemon, Golden Onion, Onion-Mushroom or Onion Soup Mix.

CHINESE VEGETABLES

1 pound fresh broccoli
1½ teaspoons vegetable oil
2 medium yellow onions, cut
    into wedges and separated
2 cloves garlic, minced
4½ teaspoons minced fresh
    ginger
8 ounces fresh spinach,
    coarsely chopped
4 stalks celery, diagonally cut
    into ½-inch pieces

8 ounces fresh snow peas *or*
1 package (6 ounces)
    thawed frozen snow peas,
    trimmed and strings
    removed
4 medium carrots, sliced
8 green onions, diagonally cut
    into thin slices
¾ cup reduced-sodium chicken
    broth
1 tablespoon reduced-sodium
    soy sauce

Cut broccoli tops into florets. Cut stalks into 2×¼-inch strips. Heat oil in wok or large nonstick skillet over high heat. Add broccoli stalks, yellow onions, garlic and ginger; stir-fry 1 minute. Add broccoli florets, spinach, celery, snow peas, carrots and green onions; toss gently. Add broth and soy sauce to vegetables; toss to coat. Bring to a boil; cover and cook 2 to 3 minutes until vegetables are crisp-tender. *Makes 4 servings*

DINER SKILLET POTATOES

1½ pounds all-purpose potatoes,
    peeled and diced
2 large red or green bell
    peppers, chopped

1 envelope LIPTON® Recipe
    Secrets® Onion Soup Mix*
2 tablespoons olive or
    vegetable oil

In large bowl, combine potatoes, bell peppers and Onion Soup Mix until evenly coated.

In 12-inch nonstick skillet, heat oil over medium heat and cook potato mixture, covered, stirring occasionally, 12 minutes. Remove cover and continue cooking, stirring occasionally, 10 minutes or until potatoes are tender. *Makes about 6 servings*

*Also terrific with Lipton® Recipe Secrets® Fiesta Herb with Red Pepper Soup Mix.

ALMOND BROCCOLI STIR–FRY

1 bunch (about 1 pound)
    broccoli
¾ cup BLUE DIAMOND®
    Chopped Natural Almonds
3 tablespoons vegetable oil
3 cloves garlic, thinly sliced

2 tablespoons soy sauce
1 tablespoon sugar
1 teaspoon grated fresh ginger
    or ¼ teaspoon ground
    ginger
1 teaspoon lemon juice

Cut broccoli into florets. Trim and peel stalks; cut on diagonal into thin slices and reserve. In large skillet or wok cook and stir almonds in oil 1 minute. Add broccoli and stir-fry until barely tender, about 2 minutes. Add garlic and stir-fry until just tender, about 1 minute. Stir in soy sauce, sugar and ginger. Continue stir-frying until sugar dissolves, about 1 minute. Add lemon juice.

Makes 4 servings

STIR–FRY RICE AND VEGETABLES

3 tablespoons vegetable oil
1 bunch green onions, white
    and green parts chopped
    separately
1 medium sweet potato,
    peeled, halved lengthwise
    and thinly sliced
1 small green bell pepper, cut
    into thin strips

2 carrots, thinly sliced
1 zucchini, thinly sliced
2 cups cooked brown rice
1 cup bean sprouts
1 cup fresh mushrooms, sliced
¼ cup honey
¼ cup soy sauce

Heat oil in wok or large, heavy skillet over medium-high heat. Stir-fry white parts of onions, sweet potato, bell pepper, carrots and zucchini until barely tender. Add rice, sprouts, mushrooms and green onion tops. Cook quickly until heated through. If necessary, add more oil. Combine honey and soy sauce in cup. Pour over mixture and stir. Serve immediately.

Makes 6 to 8 servings

Favorite recipe from **National Honey Board**

SPICY ORIENTAL GREEN BEANS

1 pound whole green beans, trimmed

2 tablespoons chopped green onions

2 tablespoons dry sherry or chicken broth

4½ teaspoons reduced-sodium soy sauce

1 teaspoon chili sauce with garlic

1 teaspoon Oriental sesame oil

1 clove garlic, minced
  Edible flowers such as pansies, violets or nasturtiums for garnish

Fill Dutch oven with water to depth of ½ inch. Bring water to a boil. Place green beans in steamer basket in Dutch oven. Cover and steam beans about 5 minutes or just until crisp-tender. Drain and set aside.

Combine green onions, sherry, soy sauce, chili sauce, sesame oil and garlic in small bowl. Spray large skillet with nonstick cooking spray; heat over medium heat. Add green beans; pour soy sauce mixture over beans. Toss well to coat. Cook 3 to 5 minutes, stirring constantly until heated through. Garnish, if desired.   *Makes 4 servings*

Spicy Oriental Green Beans

ACKNOWLEDGMENTS

The publisher would like to thank the companies and organizations listed below for the use of their recipes and photographs in this publication.

American Lamb Council

Blue Diamond Growers

Dean Foods Vegetable Company

Delmarva Poultry Industry, Inc.

Del Monte Foods

Dole Food Company, Inc.

Golden Grain/Mission Pasta

Grandma's Molasses, a division of Cadbury Beverages Inc.

Heinz U.S.A.

Holland House, a division of Cadbury Beverages Inc.

Kahlúa Liqueur

Kikkoman International Inc.

Kraft Foods, Inc.

Lawry's® Foods, Inc.

Lee Kum Kee (USA) Inc.

Thomas J. Lipton Co.

McCormick & Co., Inc.

McIlhenny Company

Minnesota Cultivated Wild Rice Council

National Cattlemen's Beef Association

National Honey Board

National Onion Association

Nestlé Food Company

Nestlé Specialty Products Company

Newman's Own, Inc.

Norseland, Inc.

North Dakota Wheat Commission

The Procter & Gamble Company

Riviana Foods Inc.

StarKist Seafood Company

Surimi Seafood Education Center

Walnut Marketing Board

Washington Apple Commission

INDEX

93